# Cyp

CW00591648

Gateway to East and West

JARROLD

# CONTENTS

*Laceworking*

# This is Cyprus

There are few countries of such manageable size that can meet so many of your holiday needs at once as Cyprus, the island of Aphrodite. Only a few hours flying time from the daily grind and you will soon understand why the goddess of love, beauty and spring sought out this corner of the earth to arise from the foaming, clear (even today!) waters of the Mediterranean.

This island, the form of which seems truly in keeping with the Olympian legend, is as if made for relaxing, playing sport, climbing about ancient ruins, lingering in tavernas and being spoilt in luxurious hotels. And above all the sun hardly ever stops shining. It even seems to enjoy warming the olive and orange groves, the ripening grapes, the sleepy villages in the hilly countryside, the monasteries hidden in the mountains and the magnificent bays.

To be in Cyprus on holiday means to live like the gods. You may choose to sunbathe, swim, sail, dive, gently rock on a fishing boat in the shallow swell; or you could walk on the peaks of the Troodos Mountains or enjoy watching the 'simple life' from the café in the village square. There is the charm of past cultures from Stone-Age Khirokitia to the Byzantine frescos of Asinou or the bustling life on the seafront at Larnaca - and all this can be experienced on the same day - or in winter a stroll on the snow-covered slopes of Olympos and a dip into the Mediterranean at temperatures almost reaching 20°C. Cyprus is well worth a visit at any time of the year.

## Geography

Cyprus, the third largest Mediterranean island, has about 780km of coastline. Geographically part of Asia, Cyprus is only 65km from the south coast of Anatolia, 95km from the Syrian coast, 380km from Egypt and 550km from the island of Crete. Two mountain ranges cross the island from east to west - the 150km-long, narrow ridge of the Pentadaktylos Mountains (Kyrenia and Karpasia) with the 1024m Kyparissovouno, and the more southerly Troodos Mountains where the highest summit of the island, Mount Olympos, is to be found. Between them stretches the wide, fertile plain of Mesaoria in the centre of which lies Nicosia. In the west it is bordered by Morphou Bay and in the east by Famagusta Bay. Apart from the capital Nicosia, all main towns are situated on the coast.

*One of the many beautiful mosaics to be found on Cyprus*

## Essential details in brief

[Information in square brackets refers to Turkish Republic of Northern Cyprus]

**Name:** *Kypriaki Dimokratia* (Greek), *Kibris Cumhuriyeti* (Turkish) - Republic of Cyprus.

**Founded:** August 16th 1960, previously British Crown Colony. [Nov. 15th 1983 Proclamation of the 'Turkish Republic of Northern Cyprus' - internationally not recognised.]

**Area:** With an area of 9251 sq. km Cyprus is the third biggest Mediterranean island. [Since 1974-75 35% of Cyprus has been claimed by the Turkish Cypriot State.] There are also two British sovereign military bases, Akrotiri and Dhekelia (256 sq. km).

**Government:** Presidential republic based on parliamentary democratic lines. At present Parliament consists of 56 members elected for 4 years. In 1985 elections: Communist Party AKEL 27.4% = 15 MPs; Democratic Party (Centre Right) 27.6% = 16 MPs; Democratic Alliance (Right) 33.5% = 19 MPs; Socialist Party EDEK (Centre Left) 11.5% = 6 MPs.
President and Head of Government: Georgios Vassiliou (Independent).

**Capital:** Nicosia (150,000 inhabitants) [North Nicosia 45,000].

**Membership:** UNO, Commonwealth, EC Association, OECD.

**Population:** 680,000. 520,200 Greek Cypriots [159,800 Turkish Cypriots in the North].

**Refugees:** Approximately 145,000 Greek Cypriots from the North [approximately 60,000 Turkish Cypriots from the South].

**Religion:** Predominantly Greek Orthodox Christians [Moslems in Turkish Cypriot zone].

**Language:** Greek [Turkish]. English widespread.

**Foreign Soldiers:** 1200 Greeks, 2300 members of UN peace-keeping force (Unficyp), British Forces. [Approx. 20,000 Turks.]

**Economy:** Intensive agriculture, manufacture of consumer goods, food-processing, tourism.

**Minerals:** Copper and iron pyrite, asbestos, gypsum.

**Exports:** Industrial products including textiles, shoes and cement; potatoes, other agricultural products (citrus fruit, fruit, wine, grapes).

**Important Trading Partners:** Arab countries, EC countries (esp. England) [Turkey].

**Imports:** Machines, vehicles and other industrial products, foodstuffs, raw materials and fuels.

# ◪ Holidays in Cyprus

In Cyprus you can really start to relax. Both the natural beauty and the Cypriot people see to that. The hotels are good, prices favourable and the service is first-rate. There is something for everyone on the menu — wines and beers are excellent, and so are the freshly pressed fruit juices and the mineral water. There is a wide selection of guided tours to the island's sights. If you are hiring a car you will find the roads of a satisfactory standard.

Sandy beaches are not only to be found in the tourist areas. Many undeveloped parts of the coastline invite you to swim, though do not expect all of the beaches to be sandy. Often you may have to cross stones and pebbles to reach the water so a pair of bathing shoes could be useful. As all the beaches slope gently down to the sea, where there are no dangerous currents and even sea urchins and jellyfish are rare, it is ideal for children.

Holidaymakers of average means are always welcome in the hotels, but more self-indulgent tourists will find a 'green version of the beach' in Limassol's luxury hotels. Here you can relax on green lawns instead of on sand, and there are wooden paths over which to make your way to the water. If salt water is not for you then most of the bigger hotels have a swimming pool.

The wonderfully warm water invites every kind of watersport. Most beach hotels have equipment for water-skiing, diving, windsurfing and rowing, or at least can inform you where it is available for hire. Of course, you can also fish in the sea but do not despair if you have little success. Owing to the relatively high salt content and low plankton levels fish stocks in the waters surrounding the island are low. Keen sailors should contact the sailing clubs in Larnaca, Limassol or Paphos. Hotels and tourist information offices will gladly supply further details.

A game of tennis in the morning or evening is not to be dismissed. Many hotels have courts but there are also sports clubs and centres where you can work up a sweat. Less exhausting is the enjoyment of a relaxing horse ride in the Troodos Mountains — a real pleasure. For the independent walker there are quiet footpaths amongst the cornfields and groves of oranges and olives. If you do not mind a steep climb the Troodos mountain range with its extensive shady woods is to be recommended. The magnificent fresh and tangy air makes it ideal walking country.

For the art-lover, historian and archaeologist Cyprus is like El Dorado. Evidence of almost 9000 years of history awaits the interested visitor.

A holiday in Cyprus is never boring!

## The Cypriot way of life

It is impossible to write in depth about the Cypriots without referring to a tragic event in their recent past. Since the division of the island in 1974 the population of the Republic of Cyprus has been almost entirely Greek. They have been separated from their Turkish Cypriot former fellow-citizens by a Demarcation Line.

It is all the more surprising to see what has been achieved in the south of the island (we are only concerned here with this part) since the division, which almost brought economic ruin. Through their hard work, business acumen and talent for organisation the Cypriots have performed a real economic miracle. Of course, to be fair, one cannot disregard the investment of foreign capital. They point out with justifiable pride the widespread integration of refugees, the considerable number of

*The donkey, the fishing boat and the street café — part of the simple life that can still be seen on Cyprus*

*Cypriot wedding preparations*

new hotels and holiday complexes, the new streets and suburbs — and yet the people have remained charming; they have not yet allowed themselves to be spoilt by progress.

In the country, where the majority of Cypriots earn their daily bread cultivating the fields, fruit plantations and vineyards, time seems to have passed more slowly. Here the visitor can still find those people who personify the Mediterranean way of life. Their weather-beaten and suntanned faces suggest that they have had to work hard, and yet they radiate an inner calmness which even the cries of their many happy children cannot disturb. The Cypriots like children — and not just their own.

The extended family is still intact here — the joyful picnics at the weekends prove it. And no traveller is allowed to pass without a *Kopiaste* — 'Come and sit down, my friend, and have a drink.' The proverbial Cypriot hospitality is genuine.

## Religion and Tradition

The Cypriots are a religious people. The prayers to the icons suggest that the belief in tradition is deeply rooted, for young and old alike. It probably brought stability and confidence to many in the centuries of oppression, even if the prayers for freedom were not heard until 1960.

The numerous celebrations and public holidays on the island have a long tradition. Whoever has experienced Carnival in Limassol, a wine festival or the Larnaca water festival *Kataklysmos* will have no doubt that the Cypriots know how to celebrate.

The strong influence of old customs on island life can be seen most vividly at a typical village wedding. On the wedding day itself several rituals have to be carried out in a particular order before the actual marriage ceremony can take place. These include: the 'highly confidential' negotiations on the part of the bridegroom's parents before the official marriage contract; preparing the hollowed-out gourds to

*Limassol Carnival*

make bottles to be filled with wine, which together with a ring-shaped bread roll serve as the invitation; the 'dance of the bridegroom's suit' or the 'dance of the wedding dress'; the ritual of laying out and dancing upon the mattress upon which later the wedding gifts will be spread; the 'last shave' which the bridegroom will perform as a bachelor (accompanied by music). During the wedding service when the priest finally says 'to love and obey' the bride steps on the bridegroom's foot, indicating that these words do not just apply to her. In order to ensure peace the newlyweds are presented with a pair of white doves after the ceremony. Only then do the actual celebrations start; these involve wine, singing and dancing and can last for days.

## Flora and Fauna

Fifty-five per cent of the island's terrain is used for agriculture. Almost seventy per cent of it is arable land which, as a result of artificial irrigation, yields several harvests a year; seventeen per cent is meadow land and pastures and thirteen per cent is dedicated to long-term fruit production, wine and citrus fruits.

Twenty per cent of the island is forested. The forests which cover both mountain ranges, the Pentadaktylos range in the north and the Troodos range in the south, consist primarily of Aleppo pines, firs, cypresses (possible origin of the island's name), cedars, planes and oaks. Great efforts towards afforestation are being made not only because of awareness of the climatic importance of forests but also due to the economic value of wood. Throughout the island the visitor will come across olive, fig, carob and almond trees.

In spring (March, April) the island resembles a gigantic carpet of blossoms. The unmistakable scent of the flowering citrus trees penetrates the whole of the countryside. In this season poppies, blue irises and wallflowers predominate together with tulips, narcissi and crown imperials. In many places meadows full of fragrant alpine violets are to be found, while several types of wild orchids brighten up the woods and undergrowth.

In summer the glistening heat bestows assorted shades of brown upon the flat plain. It is during this season that the delicious succulent sugar melons and water melons are harvested.

The first rain in October quickly covers the dried-out earth with a delicate green which is closely followed by autumn narcissi, grape hyacinth and anemones along with the yellow, white and scarlet crowfoot.

The most noteworthy animal on Cyprus is the moufflon, a wild mountain sheep with magnificent curled horns. However, it is only to be found in an inaccessible part of the Paphos forests (Troodos Mountains). Snakes used to be a major problem for the island but nowadays most of them are extinct. On the other hand you very often come across the fascinating chameleon, especially between the hot stones of the ruins on ancient sites. As well as turtles, tree frogs and toads there are numerous hedgehogs, and hares and foxes in the mountains.

Among the birds feature peregrine falcons and kestrels, in addition to the imperial eagle, two species of vulture and, in the marshy areas, herons. In winter woodcock are a sought-after quarry. Cranes flying in tight formation across the island offer a marvellous sight — unlike storks, flamingos and swallows they never make a stop. Bee-keeping is widespread and the holidaymaker should not leave without tasting the delicious Cyprus honey.

*Fields of Cyprus in springtime*

**Signposts of History and Culture**

| Period | History | Culture |
|---|---|---|
| **7500-3900 B.C.**<br>*Early Stone Age* | First settlements on Cyprus | Khirokitia 7000-6000<br>Sotira 4500-3750 |
| **3900-2300**<br>*Chalcolithic period* | | Erimi |
| **2300-1900**<br>*Early Bronze Age* | Beginning of Cypriot copper mining, its working and trade. | Early Cypriot period. Kition |
| **1900-1625**<br>*Middle Bronze Age* | From 1500 Egyptian domination. | Middle Cypriot period. Enkomi. |
| **1625-1050**<br>*Late Bronze Age* | From 1400 predominance of Mycenaean culture. About 1200 Trojan wars. Greek heroes said to have appeared on island and founded several towns. In Paphos the legendary priest-king Cinyras rules. Aegean colonisation. | Late Cypriot period. Beginning of Salamis and temple culture of Ayia Irini. Horned god of Enkomi. |
| **1050-725**<br>*Iron Age* | Period of kingdoms. Cyprus has 200,000 inhabitants. Immigrant Phoenicians found own colony. Assyrian rule. | Cypro-geometric period |
| **725-475** | Golden Age for Cyprus divided up into 9 city kingdoms. Most powerful are Salamis, Paphos, Amathus and Kition. Egyptian rule until 525, followed by Persian. | Cypro-archaic period. Two-tone and borderless ceramics. Kings' graves and palaces in Tamassos, Vouni and Salamis. |
| **475-325** | 435-373 King Evagoras of Salamis. | Cypro-classical period. |
| **325-58**<br>*Hellenistic Period* | 323 Death of Alexander the Great.<br>294-58 Ptolemaic rule. | So-called Tombs of the Kings, Paphos. |
| **58 B.C.-A.D. 326**<br>*Roman Period* | 58 B.C. Cyprus becomes Roman province with Paphos the capital. A.D. 45 St Paul introduces Christianity. His companion Barnabas dies a martyr in Salamis. A.D. 116 Jewish revolt. | Temple of Apollo. Theatre and houses of Eustolios in Curium. Mosaics in Curium, Paphos and other towns. |

| Period | History | Culture |
|---|---|---|
| **326-1191**<br>*Byzantine Period* | 431 Council of Ephesus, beginning of independent autocephalic church of Cyprus. 632-965 Arab attacks in wake of conflicts between Byzantium and Islam. Desecration of ancient sites. From then on Byzantine rule. Development of important trading. | 327 Stavrovouni monastery. 5th century monastery of St Barnabas. 7th century mosaic in Kiti. 10th century church in Peristerona. Monasteries of Kykko, Makheras, Chrysorroyiatissa. |
| **1191-1489**<br>*Rule of Lusignans* | Period of Crusades. 1191 Richard I (Lionheart) conquers the island and hands it over to the Templars. 1192 Guy de Lusignan establishes feudal system and Roman Catholicism. 1359-69 Peter I. Peak of Lusignans' power. 1453 Fall of Constantinople. | Cathedral of St Sophia, Nicosia. Expansion of Byzantine fortifications of Kyrenia, St Hilarion, and Buffavento. St Nicholas Cathedral in Famagusta. Kolossi Castle. |
| **1489-1573**<br>*Venetian Rule* | Military and commercial exploitation of the island. | |
| **1573-1878**<br>*Turkish Rule* | Restoration of Greek Orthodox Church. Turkish Occupation. | Cathedrals of Nicosia and Famagusta become Mosques. |
| **1878-1960**<br>*British Rule* | 1878 British-Turkish secret agreement. England charged with occupation and administration of Cyprus. 1914 Turkey enters First World War; England annexes Cyprus. 1923 Turkey gives up claims to Cyprus in treaty of Lausanne. 1925 Cyprus becomes Crown Colony. 1960 Cyprus becomes independent. | |
| **Aug. 16 1960**<br>*Republic of Cyprus* | 1963, 1964, 1967 Disturbances between Greek and Turkish population. July 20 1974 Turkish military intervention. Feb. 13 1975 Declaration of Federated Turkish State of Cyprus. Aug. 3 1977 Makarios III dies. Nov. 15 1983 Proclamation of Turkish Republic of Northern Cyprus. | |

#  History and Legend

Cyprus, torn between East and West, has a stormy past. You can best experience its history by being there yourself and visiting Kalavassos-Tenta or Khirokitia.

## Neolithic period

Up until the discovery of *Kalavassos-Tenta*, where man had built settlements as early as 7500 B.C., the oldest known village on Cyprus had been *Khirokitia*. It belonged to that period when man turned his back on nomadic life in order to settle down as a farmer and cattle breeder. Khirokitia ranks as one of the most significant Stone Age settlements excavated so far. Between 7000 and 6000 B.C. the tightly packed, beehive-like round stone buildings appeared, with their round roofs made of dried clay tiles. Life on the island must have been hard in those days and the Stone Age settlers had nothing available to combat the forces of nature other than the various implements found at Khirokitia: hand grinders made from large stones from the river, stone sickles, spinning wheels and weaving weights, and containers made of wood, bone, stone, leather or pumpkin skins. The round hut (Gk. *tholos*) offered protection against the wind and rain, but under the floor on which its Stone Age inhabitants sat lurked the dead ancestors who could come back at any time, so they used to lay heavy stones on their chests! In spite of this life was not safe, for over this primitive early world, of which little is known, reigned the Great Mother who gave birth to all life and devoured it all, and who could only be appeased by human sacrifice. The numerous graves belonging to children found under some tholoi lead to the conclusion that even child sacrifice was common in Khirokitia, and the remaining skeletons suggest that the inhabitants of this settlement were rarely older than 30 or 35 years.

## Chalcolithic period

The next stage in Cypriot history is *Erimi*, a settlement founded about 3800 B.C. near the fortress of Kolossi. The numerous idols that have been excavated here suggest that a mother deity was still worshipped, who gradually emerged out of the shadows of primordial anonymity to become a female image of exaggerated sexuality. This powerful goddess of early matriarchal society still had the power, a millennium later, to attract men and subjugate them as her servants and attendants.

Even so she consorted with the Telchins, dwarfs equipped with magical powers who according to legend had totally transformed life on the island.

The ancient legends state that the Telchins were actually magical demons who had come to the island long ago. Perhaps the mysterious appearance of these 'men of the sea' in various guises reflects a distant memory of the first colonisers of the island who came across the sea and brought with them the art of working metal. The original working of the copper reserves on Cyprus must have begun about 2300 B.C.

## Trade expands

In the second millennium B.C. the island became an important trading place in the eastern Mediterranean, which gave it the complimentary reputation in the known world at that time of having reached an enviable level of civilisation.

From the 16th century B.C. Mycenaean culture developed to the west of Cyprus

In the east and south the rebellious Hittite kingdom and the reinforced New Kingdom of Egypt opposed each other. Cyprus was for a while subject to Egypt, without its own development being stifled — in fact the opposite occurred. In the late Bronze Age, due to increased copper production, the island experienced thriving and unbroken economic development and began for the first time to play a significant role as mediator in the cultural exchange between East and West.

## Bronze Age

The development process of the prehistoric Cypriot can best be followed in the Nicosia Museum, beginning with the Early Bronze Age and progressing in the most remarkable ways. For then as now man expressed the world, as he perceived and understood it, in his art.

Of unusual bulging shape, the jugs and amphoras from about 2000 B.C. resemble creatures of the sea and have strange tube-like protuberances. Following the Middle Bronze Age, during which vessels suddenly were provided with small graceful bases, and after the period of decorated Cypro-Mycenaean ceramics of the 14th and 13th centuries B.C., the wonderful examples of so-called 'borderless' ceramics were to be found in the Cypro-archaic period of the 7th century B.C. Liberated from the limitations of an ornamental border the magnificent mythical creatures flew, galloped and stretched across the surface of the vessels. It was as if something had finally broken free. But the surprising thing is that man, who at the beginning of the first millennium B.C. had shown himself to be so imaginative and at the same time a keen observer of the plant and animal kingdom, still perceived himself as a half-blind creature. At least this is the impression one gets from the sacerdotal army of clay worshippers from the temple at *Ayia Irini*. The majority of the figures have their eyes closed below their peaked helmets. Their faces bearing stern expressions are piously raised, their gestures clumsy and their posture stiff. After the dramatic explosion of form in their ceramics these strange puppets are almost disappointing; yet you still have the feeling when you study these creatures more closely that behind their closed eyelids they are imagining something beautiful.

A few steps further in this jewel of a museum — three, four hundred years later in time — these beautiful thoughts are superseded by the gentle, precociously superior smile of Ionic knowledge. Eventually even this knowledge explodes and he is finally here — man himself. The image may only be in stone or marble but it is so free, so fearless, so full of potential that in spite of the museum's atmosphere and his tired feet the observer is overwhelmed by so much reality. The omnipotent Great Mother ceases to exist. The childhood of the human race is irrevocably past. The whole world consciousness had completely changed in the first millennium B.C. What had happened?

## Trojan heroes on Cyprus

About 1200 B.C. one of the most momentous events of world history began — the Aegean migration. Indo-Germanic hordes penetrated the lands around the Eastern Mediterranean and drove part of the population of Greece into Asia Minor and onto the Aegean islands. It was through this violent movement that the Aegean became part of the Greek world that we know today. Caught up in this exodus the Greeks came to Cyprus which until now had always been colonised by the East. This event

is preserved in the legend which tells how the towns in Cyprus were founded by the heroes of the Trojan War. The town of Nea Paphos is said to have been founded by the shipwrecked King Agapenor of Tegea; according to tradition Lapithos dates back to the Laconian Praxanor and Soli was founded by Acamas, the son of Theseus. Teucer, one of King Telamon's sons, is portrayed as responsible for founding the most important town of this period — Salamis. At the same time Cinyras, the legendary king of Cyprus, is said to have been a pronounced Grecophile and to have sent Agamemnon the very suit of armour that was described in detail in the Iliad. The Greeks were not, of course, the only settlers on Cyprus. About 900 B.C. Phoenicians returned and founded their own centres of commerce to which, to a great extent, the island owed its flourishing economic success in the prosperous period between 700 and 475 B.C. However, it was the Greek influence that predominated eventually. East and West had united on Cyprus and it was not long before the oppressive shadows of the Great Mother faded.

## Aphrodite

Long before the time of the mythical Cinyras, Aphrodite had already risen from the sea off the coast of Cyprus. Strictly speaking a matriarch without a father she was considered, after Cyprus's love affair with Greece, to be the daughter of Zeus. Aphrodite had driven away her predecessor *Ischtar/Astarte* and seen to it that the island continued to be ruled by a female goddess — and what a goddess she was! Aphrodite, or Cypris as she was also named, after the place of her birth, was no longer the awesome black and white mother but lover, temptress, the most beautiful woman of all, who according to Hesiod bewitched men 'with the whispering of young girls, with infatuating laughter and fun, with sweet desire'. Aphrodite came in order to enchant and bring joy — even the immortals welcomed her enthusiastically. The enthusiasm was mutual. Aphrodite's escapades run to several chapters in the Olympians' 'Chronique Scandaleuse'. Her realm is that of love on earth as in heaven, and when Zeus, smiling indulgently, forbade her to participate in the affairs of men with the words, 'my little daughter, your business is not affairs of war — concern yourself instead with the charming affairs of marriage', she reacted according to the lustful laws of her own principles by being unfaithful to her own husband, and predictably with the god of war, Ares. Aphrodite hated marriage. Hephaistos, the cuckolded husband, succeeded in catching the love-crazed couple in an invisible net of metallic threads spun around the den of sin and in bringing them before the Olympian Court. Yet he was to be ridiculed again. The gods received his anger with frivolous jokes and Homeric laughter.

## Aphrodite on Cyprus

After this embarrassing affair Ares disappeared to Thrace; 'But the smiling Aphrodite went to Kypros to the grove of Paphos and the altar scented with incense,' in order to console herself with new lovers at her birthplace, her favourite island. This is where her illustrious love life began.

Pygmalion, an earlier god of the island, was one of the first who fell in love with her. According to the myth which describes him as a king of the island, he had fallen in love with a naked ivory figure of the goddess.

*Left: Birthplace of Aphrodite*

Next was *Cinyras,* Pygmalion's grandson, the legendary national hero and priest king of Cyprus from pre-Greek times, and who appeared in Homer's Iliad as a great friend of the Achaeans. Cinyras is said to have introduced mining and metal-working along with all kinds of tools, wool-weaving and sheep-rearing to the island, and to have ranked as an equal with the gods. Above all, the myth depicts him as the handsome, god-like, anointed and adorned friend and favourite of Aphrodite, and the star of her favour is said to have shone for a long time on his family. In any case the rule of the Cinyrades stretched into many centuries, and the exceptional status of the priest kings of Paphos is evident from a Roman inscription in which Paphos was referred to as 'the spiritual head of all Cypriot towns'.

However, as Aphrodite turned her irresistible eyes away from Cinyras, the father, to his son Adonis, who had meanwhile grown up into a magnificent youth, Ares, crazed with jealousy, returned from Thrace to put a nasty end to this latest romance, in the forest. Transformed into a snorting boar he fatally wounded Adonis from whose blood, so legend has it, the roses of Cyprus grew. In contrast, from the tears of the inconsolable Aphrodite grew the anemones which cover the whole island like a pinkish-red and white carpet when it is her Holy Day.

The accounts of the infamous orgiastic ceremonies on the night of the birth of Cypris are sparse and contradictory. These were undoubtedly of an erotic nature. There are stories of sacral prostitution; the initiation of young boys by priestesses; the island's virgins who, seeking to prove their loyalty to the goddess of love, gave

*Khirokitia*

*Limassol: The Castle*

themselves nightly to strangers on the seashore. All of this belongs to tradition rather than researched history. At any rate the daughters of the island were well acquainted with the art of love, and the scented blossoms and tingling foam of Cyprus's beauty created a sensual atmosphere in which poets vied to outdo each other in their praise. In Euripides' *Maenad* the chorus sings: 'Oh let me go to Cyprus to greet Aphrodite with her erotic charms which steal men's hearts.'

The domination of the goddess of love has, over the centuries, had a decisive influence on island life, and her radiance was so great that the glory of her shrine in Paphos reached a new zenith under the Romans. When its buildings were destroyed by an earthquake Augustus had them rebuilt. And when a new goddess, the Virgin Mary, moved in to Cyprus's holy places, the artists of the island adorned the image of the new chaste maiden with the roses, anemones and white doves of their beloved Cypris.

Several customs, such as the biggest festival on the island today, the so-called 'Kataklysmos', the Larnaca water festival, are reminiscent of the ancient celebrations of Aphrodite. The ancient fertility rite of splashing each other with water is kept alive here in honour of 'Our Lady of the Sea'. Even that noble contest during which the village bards compete around the campfire for the laurel wreath, awarded for the most eloquent rendering of the most beautiful ballad, is supposed to have been originally introduced in honour of Aphrodite.

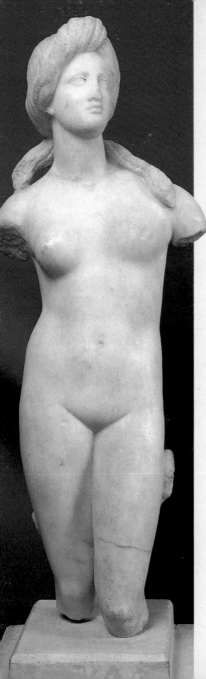

# APHRODITE

## The Myth

It was not merely coincidence that Aphrodite rose out of the foam on the shores of Cyprus. Since time immemorial a female deity has been worshipped here — the Great Mother, who ruled over life and death, was idolised by primitive matriarchal society throughout the continent of Asia Minor.

For a long time Aphrodite was worshipped in a variety of shapes and forms and not all of them reflecting her beauty and gentleness, some being reminiscent of her terrifying predecessor. She was called *Melainis*, the black one, or even *Androphonos*, the mankiller, among other names.

Idols to a female deity were found in the Stone Age settlements of Khirokitia and Erimi (6000 and 3000 B.C. respectively). Perhaps the strange cross-shaped idol represents the mystical marriage of the mother goddess.

The late Bronze Age clay idol (14th—12th century B.C.) with the fearsome animal head shows the influence of ancient oriental religious figures in Cyprus. It is hard to believe that this primitive goddess reappeared a few centuries later under the Greeks as the most beautiful and enchanting goddess of all.

The Virgin Mary followed as her successor and assumed many characteristics of the pagan goddess.

 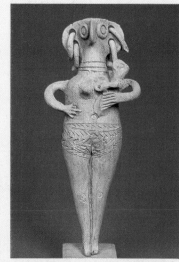

*Bronze and Stone Age idols found on Cyprus, possibly predecessors of Aphrodite.*

## Byzantine period

In Paphos — naturally! — the apostle Paul appeared in A.D. 45. The outraged disciples of Aphrodite tied the 'heretic' to a column and flogged him. This stubborn missionary had more success with the Roman Proconsul Sergius Paulus who had meanwhile settled in the town. He was willingly converted and thereby made Cyprus into the first country to be ruled by a Christian, although the heathen temples of Paphos and Soli were still in use until the 4th century. But around the period of the Council of Nicea (325) the island already had three bishops, and towards the end of the century it was completely Christian. From A.D. 330 Cyprus was under Byzantine administration.

Cyprus was to belong to this new power, the Byzantine Empire, for almost 900 years. To understand how the islanders (apart, of course, from the Turks) still regard themselves as unquestionably Greek today, you need to look back to this period. The essential spirit, culture and national character of the island up to the present day have been formed through the centuries of life in the Graeco-Christian world of Byzantium. Even the sharp division between the small circle of the educated and the landowning classes and the vast mass of the rural population goes back to that period. Wealthy landowners, high-ranking officials and clergy evidently enjoyed their full share of the economic prosperity of the early Byzantine period. However, the vast majority of the population in the country consisted of farmers who, being tenants, were just as tied as the craftsmen in the towns who were forced to offer their services.

## Richard the Lionheart and the Templars

Politically the fate of Byzantium is essentially also that of the island. The expansionism of the Islamic tribes of Arabia, which first manifested itself in A.D. 630 with the attack by a troop of Bedouins on a Byzantine fort on the Dead Sea, brought about the 800-year struggle against Byzantium which ended with the fall of Constantinople and brought three dark centuries of continual warfare to Cyprus (A.D. 632–965). The island had to pay dearly for the strategic importance it held from the very beginning between the two world religions.

About A.D. 850 the external political situation had shifted in favour of Byzantium and the next wave of conquerors to arrive in Cyprus came not from the Arabian desert but from Europe. The Crusaders had been mobilising there to drive the Turks out of the Holy Land. Strange-sounding names sprang up on Cyprus's shores — in 1191 Richard the Lionheart arrived; the Templars came and went; the Knights of St John remained. When Emperor Frederick II landed on the island in 1228, after his crusade had been repeatedly postponed, he was greeted by his former 'neighbours', for Cyprus had been firmly in European hands since 1192.

## The Kingdom of the Lusignans

The English king Richard the Lionheart had come as a Crusader to Cyprus in 1191, to save his stranded bride Berengaria of Navarre from the threat of imprisonment by the Byzantine emperor of the island, Isaac Comnenus. This precipitated a battle from which Richard the Lionheart emerged as the new ruler of the island. However, the island was too great a financial burden so he gave it to one of the French aristocracy from Poitou—Guy de Lusignan, who moved here in 1192. This was Cyprus's first period of political independence. For 300 years it remained a united

*Hadji Georghakis House — the oldest Turkish building in Nicosia*

kingdom under the Lusignans, a time of cultural and economic splendour. It was the most easterly bastion of Western Christianity, a staging post for the Crusaders and a commercial centre in East-West trade. Money poured in, people came and went and everywhere frantic building work was taking place. This show of splendour by the rulers seemed almost fairytale-like to passing pilgrims. And while the Crusaders were defeated and the last outpost of Christianity fell in 1291 in Akko (Palestine), the island enjoyed power, wealth and cultural activity of new heights. In Famagusta the Lusignans were crowned kings of Jerusalem and here they indulged their most exotic tastes.

After the fall of Akko a hotch-potch of the most cunning sea captains, businessmen and bankers from the Levant mixed with Christian refugees. The street where the old inns used to be was inhabited by the consuls of Genoa, Venice, Pisa, Ancona, Montpellier, Narbonne and Barcelona. The confusion of foreign tongues in the narrow street was truly Babylonian. The wealth was so immense that a trader with the profit from just one shop was able to build the formidable Church of St Peter and St Paul, and another businessman bought a tiara for his daughter's wedding that was more valuable than all the jewellery of the Queen of France. The barons passed their time with sport, court intrigue and love affairs. A certain count of Jaffa and Ashkelon had a servant for each pair of his 500 hunting dogs. While Famagusta's courtesans often amassed private fortunes of up to 100,000 ducats, so it was said, the city rulers still had enough money left to pay off their sins by building churches in the pure Gothic style of their French homeland.

## Turkish period

The Crusades were Cyprus's glory, but also its destiny. When the star of the Lusignans faded and the Venetian Republic succeeded in acquiring their lucrative estate, the island still maintained its key position between East and West for another 90 years. But the expansionist drive of the Turks was unstoppable.

Constantinople had fallen in 1453. By 1481 the frontiers of the Ottoman Empire had reached Armenia and the Taurus in the East, and Save and Belgrade in Europe. In March 1570 the long-awaited blow fell. 'We demand that you hand over Cyprus either voluntarily or under force'. This was the ultimatum given by the Sultan Selim II — Sultan of Ottoman, Emperor of the Turks, Lord of Lords, King of Kings, Shadow of God, Master of Paradise on Earth and Jerusalem — to the Venetians in Famagusta, and which provoked one of the bloodiest and most heroic defensive battles in world history.

On August 8th 1571 he triumphantly marched into the ruins of Famagusta. The Republic of San Marco surrendered Cyprus to the Ottoman Empire on March 7th 1573. The Gothic cathedrals were turned into Mosques and the Latin dominance of Cyprus was over. For centuries Cyprus fell into poverty and oblivion.

## Modern Cyprus

In 1878 the British succeeded the Turks as rulers of the island, initially as tenants. But when in 1914 the Ottoman Empire entered the First World War on the side of Germany and the central European powers, Britain annexed Cyprus.

From the beginning the colonial intent was clear. 'Cyprus is the key to Western Asia' wrote the Prime Minister, Disraeli, to Queen Victoria. In fact the British had acquired an ideal base for controlling the sea route to India, and for exerting political and military influence in the Middle East. In the 80 years or more that they ruled the island they contributed greatly to Cyprus's re-entry into the modern world after centuries of stagnation. They built streets and introduced irrigation schemes, re-afforested depleted woodlands and carried out economic reforms. Yet despite all these improvements considerable burdens and restrictions were imposed on the population.

Up to 1914 the Sultan, who was *de jure* sovereign of the island as before, received huge rents. Even after the Cypriots formally became British subjects in 1917, and Cyprus a Crown Colony in 1925, little changed. The political control, the pressures which stemmed from colonial administrative rule and high taxation, the lack of self-determination, the feeling of being economically exploited, all gave rise to increasing discontent. The call for unity with Greece, *Enosis*, which goes back to the end of the 19th century, was becoming louder.

The colonial rulers soon exploited this and played the Greek Cypriot majority off against the Turkish Cypriot minority. Greek and Turkish nationalist groups developed, and sought the division of the population along ethnic lines.

The Second World War, in which 20,000 Cypriot volunteers served in the British army, brought a certain calm to the tension on Cyprus which had first exploded in an uprising against the British in 1931. Towards the end of the war the British

*The main square of Nicosia*

passed a few reforms, but the increasing military importance of their 'unsinkable aircraft carrier' in the Mediterranean prevented them from considering giving up Cyprus.

In 1950 Archbishop Makarios III became the new leader of the Greek Orthodox Church in Cyprus and began the real struggle for independence. Makarios the diplomat and politician knew how to put pressure on Britain with the help of the United Nations. This resulted in his banishment to the Seychelles.

In 1955 the conflict assumed international proportions when EOKA (National Organisation of Cypriot Combatants) under the leadership of General Grivas Dhigenis took up the armed struggle against the British. Great Britain wanted to keep its colony, Greece wanted unity *(Enosis),* Turkey sought the division of Cyprus *(Taksim)* and the USA was concerned about the south-eastern flank of NATO, for Athens and Ankara were threatening to attack each other to protect their national interests.

With the signing of an agreement in Zurich and London a solution was found, and in 1960 Cyprus became an independent republic. However, her sovereignty was limited by Greek and Turkish rights of intervention and by their contingents of armed forces, together with the retention of British military bases.

The original dreams of Enosis and Taksim were not fulfilled. The balance of power between both nationalities was embodied in an ingenious constitutional system. All government bodies were divided up in the ratio of 70:30 and the members of Parliament stood for particular constituencies drawn up according to nationality. However, the early co-operation between Greek and Turkish Cypriots was soon at an end. It was the suggestion of Archbishop Makarios III, president of the new republic, to change the constitutional system (which had never been democratically approved) in favour of the Greek Cypriot majority that led to bloody disturbances. The Turkish Cypriots resigned from the communal committees and the two population groups physically separated themselves. Makarios succeeded in bringing UN peace-keeping forces to Cyprus in order to prevent future clashes. They are still stationed here today.

However, some Greek Cypriots did not support Makarios's policies. The rejection of Enosis was an unforgivable betrayal. In the early 1970s General Grivas took up the struggle again with the newly formed EOKA-B. This time Makarios and his state were to be overthrown. The president barely escaped three assassination attempts. After the death of Grivas the National Guard, controlled by the military junta in Athens, tried to succeed where EOKA-B had failed. On July 15th 1974 they stormed the presidential palace. Makarios escaped through a back door, and via a British military base got out of the country. On July 20th Turkish troops occupied the north and north-east of the island 'to protect Turkish Cypriots'. The consequences were unspeakable suffering, as people were forced to flee their homes.

Makarios returned to a divided country with a demarcation line guarded by UN troops. This situation has not changed. The Greek Cypriots continue to demand a united state with the possibility of two autonomous regions. The Turkish Cypriots wanted to be one nation and not an ethnic minority and on March 12th 1975 declared the Federated Turkish State of Cyprus. On November 15th 1983 they reinforced the division of the island by proclaiming the 'Turkish Republic of Northern Cyprus', which is not recognised by international law.

*Right: Fig Tree Bay*

##  Food and Drink

Cypriot cuisine is a product of the country's history — it combines Greek, Turkish and Levantine influences. It is well worth missing, just for once, the international dishes that are exquisitely prepared in the hotels, in order to discover the delights of the taverna. You will not regret it.

No menu is complete without *Mesedes*, often referred to in the singular as *Meze*. In Greece it is a first course, in Cyprus a main course, though better described as an adventure. Meze can consist of up to thirty different delicacies and can be served hot or cold. There are fish and meat Meze. Meze can include:

| | |
|---|---|
| *Taramosalata* | a dip of strongly spiced smoked fish roe |
| *Hiromeri* | smoked Cyprus ham |
| *Melintzanosalata* | aubergine salad |
| *Kapari* | marinated capers |
| *Karaoli Wrasti* | cooked snails |
| *Psari Saworo* | fish in a piquant sauce |
| *Tallaturi* | dip of yoghurt and cucumber |
| *Mungra* | marinated cauliflower |
| *Elies Tsakistes* | green olives |
| *Oktapodi Ksioato* | marinated octopus |
| *Salatina* | pork in lemon and wine vinegar jelly |
| *Manitaria Krasata* | mushrooms in wine |
| *Keffedakia* | spicy fried fish balls |
| *Hummi Kopanisti* | chick-pea puree with olive oil & parsley |
| *Sheftalia* | grilled minced meat balls |
| *Halloumi* | goat's cheese, grilled, fried or fresh |
| *Fetta* | sharp cheese made from goat's milk |
| *Dolmas* | vine leaves stuffed with rice & minced meat |
| *Tavas* | meat roasted in a clay pot with onions |
| *Moussakas* | sort of pie made with minced meat, herbs, aubergines and other vegetables, baked in oven |
| *Stifado* | beef or veal stewed with onions and flavoured with cinnamon |
| *Skordalia* | garlic bread sauce |
| *Tahinosalata* | sesame sauce |

. . . and there is hardly a dish which does not contain plenty of garlic.

There are also, of course, many dishes with which we are familiar. You can find a suggested menu on page 29 which you may like to try yourself.

*Figs, wine and grapes — all Cyprus produce*

# Suggested menu

*For 4 people*

### Dolmades (stuffed vine leaves)

350 g minced meat, ½ cup long-grain rice, 2 onions, 2 tomatoes, a sprig of parsley, ½ cup oil, ½ cup lemon juice, black pepper, dried mint, 2 packets vine leaves (cabbage leaves if unavailable).

Place the vine or cabbage leaves in lukewarm water, finely chop onions, tomatoes and parsley and mix with the meat and washed rice. Season with salt, pepper, mint and ¼ of lemon juice. Shake the vine leaves dry, stuff them, roll them up very carefully and fold the tops, then place them in a casserole making sure they are tightly packed. Pour on oil and remainder of lemon juice. Weigh them down with a plate, place over heat and cook for 30 minutes on a low flame until the liquid is absorbed. Serve cold.

### Halloumi (grilled goat's cheese)

Cut the cheese into ½" slices and grill on both sides.

### Afelia (pork marinated in wine)

1.3 kg neck of pork, 2 tablespoons coriander, ½ cup dry red wine, salt, black peppercorns.

Wash the meat and cut into cubes. Crush the coriander and peppercorns and mix with the meat and wine. Leave to marinate for 4 to 5 hours. Heat the oil in a pan. Quickly fry the drained pieces of meat and then pour over the marinade, add salt and cook over a low heat.

### Pourgouri (wheat pilaff)

2 cups cracked wheat, 3 cups water, ½ cup oil, 3 onions, 2 ripe tomatoes, salt, black pepper.

Let the onions cook gently in the oil and add peeled, finely chopped tomatoes. Season with salt and pepper. Add the water (or stock) and cook for a few minutes. Add the cracked wheat and cook on a low heat for 30 minutes. Remove from the heat, cover the pan with a cloth and the lid and allow it to stand for a few minutes.

## Wine and other drinks

Richard the Lionheart is supposed to have said: 'I must return to Cyprus so I can sample its wine again,' and Sultan Selim II is said to have ordered the conquest of Cyprus after he had drunk 'Commandaria'. That was a long time ago, but whatever his taste the wine-lover of today will not be disappointed.

The white wine drinker can choose from the dry *Aphrodite*, *Keo Hock*, *Fair Lady*, the light sparkling *White Bellapais* or the sweeter *St. Panteleimon*. For the red wine drinker there are *Othello*, *Afames*, *Dark Lady*, *Olympos Claret* or *Keo Claret*. The rosé wines such as *Rosella*, *Rose ETKO*, *Rosita* or *Rose Sodap* are excellent. The best-known wine, however, is the sweet dessert wine *Commandaria*.

Cyprus sherry, brandy and ouzo are not to be dismissed, and we must not forget the thirst-quenching beer which is brewed on the island, the delicious fruit juices and the excellent mineral water.

# Hints for your holiday

## The Cypriot people

The Cypriots are not only polite, they are charming. They do everything to make the visitor's stay as pleasant as possible and they are genuinely pleased if you like being on their island. In the countryside it is not unusual to be offered coffee, ouzo or even a meal. Turning down such an opportunity would not only be insulting, it would be a mistake, for there is no better way of getting to know what people are really like than by sitting down for a chat.

The island population is very pious, and more conservative where morality is concerned than Northern Europeans tend to be. Visitors should show respect for their customs. When visiting churches and monasteries suitable clothing should be worn. If you go on a sightseeing trip it would be better to wear long trousers than shorts, and take a jacket to cover bare arms and shoulders.

Topless bathing is tolerated on public beaches but it is forbidden to sunbathe in the nude.

The Cypriot girls appear very shy, whereas the young men are very attentive towards female tourists travelling alone. This attention may be seen as pleasant or unnecessary but it is seldom troublesome, as these Don Juans are certainly interested but not usually a real nuisance.

When taking photographs of people exercise your discretion — it is far better to ask permission first.

# Where to go and what to see

## Nicosia Greek: Lefkosia (Southern part) Alt. 163 m; Pop. 150,000

The capital of the Republic of Cyprus lies in the middle of the fertile plain of Mesaoria. Being situated far inland it can get very hot here in summer: 40-44°C is not unusual. Fortunately the breezy heights of the Troodos Mountains are visible. The Kyrenia Mountains are also close by but they are out of bounds for Nicosia's 150,000-strong Greek population, as is the northern part of their town. Nicosia has been a divided city since the Turkish invasion in the summer of 1974. The Green Line (Demarcation Line) relentlessly carves up the whole town from east to west, from the Roccas Bastion to the Flatro Bastion through the fortified circle of the old town, with its barricades, sand bags, rusty oil drums and abandoned houses. Taking photographs is forbidden. It is guarded by both Greek and Turkish soldiers who keep their distance from the blue helmets of the UN peace-keeping troops. One cannot help thinking of the Berlin Wall, except that on Cyprus they have not been quite so thorough.

And yet today Nicosia is a lively modern city. New building developments are consuming more and more of the surrounding land. Nicosia is the seat of the President of the Republic and of the Archbishop of the Orthodox Church. The HQ of the UN peace-keeping force is situated here. The presence of big banking and business concerns, foreign embassies, modern hotels and office blocks is evidence that at least the Greek Cypriot part of the town has not lost any of its international importance as the country's centre of political and economic activity. Only the visitor to the old town, with its maze of narrow streets surrounded by the mighty walls of the Venetian fortress, will sometimes think that time has stood still. Nicosia is a city of contrasts.

Until 1974 Nicosia was the first port of call for most visitors to Cyprus. Nowadays the airport is only used by UN troops owing to its proximity to the Demarcation Line. If you are staying on the coast then you should spend at least one day visiting the island's capital.

*Nicosia with the Municipality*

##  The History of Nicosia

It is generally accepted that there was a settlement as far back as the 3rd c. B.C. on the spot where Nicosia stands today. Certainly, Leukos, the son of Ptolemy I Soter, was already actively engaged in building here in the 3rd c. B.C. The name Lefkosia is derived from his name. In the period that followed, Lefkosia's growth was overshadowed by that of the ports. Its regeneration began with the Arab raids of A.D. 648-965 on the coastal region.

The town, known as Nicosia since the 12th c., reached its heyday under the rule of the Lusignans (1192-1489). It had already become the island's capital by the Byzantine period, and now expanded over a 14-km radius. By the end of the 15th c. the population had reached 50,000 and there were 250 churches.

Not even two devastating earthquakes and the destruction and pillage perpetrated by the Genoese (1373) and Mameluks (1426) had any more than a temporary effect on the importance and prosperity of the city's ruling class. During the period of Venetian rule the defensive walls were extended (1567-1570), and they are still for the most part intact today. Yet even they were no match for the attacks of the Turkish army. After a seven-week siege the city fell to the Turks — 20,000 of the population were said to have been massacred.

The 300 years of Turkish rule left the mark of Islam on the Christian buildings: the Cathedral of St Sophia acquired two minarets and became *Selimiye Mosque*; the church of St Nicholas became *Bedestan*, a textile bazaar. The British flag was raised over Nicosia in 1878. Not until 1960 were the Cypriots finally able to call Nicosia their own capital for the first time. But four years later the city was to be violently divided into Greek and Turkish sectors.

## The Old Town

**Laiki Yitonia** ①. In 1983 this part was restored, retaining the character of the old town. Good bars and restaurants

*Archbishop's Palace, Nicosia*

are to be found together with many souvenir shops. The *Levendis Museum* ② of medieval history, opened in 1988, is situated on the outskirts of this quarter.

**Ayia Phaneromeni** ③, a church built in 1872, has a remarkable 17th c. iconostasis.

**Archbishop's Palace** ④, completed in 1960 for Independence. Makarios III lived here. His statue was erected in front of the palace in 1987. From here

Korais Street leads directly to the impressive *Liberation Monument* ⑤. The north side of the palace adjoins the church of St John, *Ayios Ioannis* ⑥, which was originally built as part of a Benedictine monastery in the 15th c.; its present form, however, dates from the 17th c. The partly restored 18th c. wall paintings are worth seeing. Above the west doorway can be seen the Lusignan coat of arms. Immediately to the west of the church the *Byzantine*

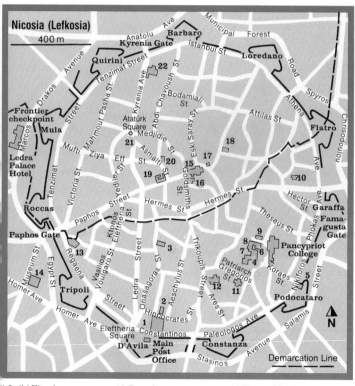

1 Laiki Yitonia
2 Levendis Museum
3 Ayia Phaneromeni
4 Archbishop's Palace
5 Liberation Monument
6 Ayios Ioannis
7 Byzantine Museum
8 Museum of Folk Art
9 Monument to the
  Struggle for Freedom

10 Panayia
   Khrysaliniotissa
11 Hadji Georghakis K.
   House
12 Omerye Mosque
13 Maronite Quarter

14 Cyprus Museum
15 St Sophia (mosque)
16 St Nicholas (Bedestan)
17 Sultan Mahmut
   Library
18 Stone Museum
19 Beuyük Han
20 Kumarçilar Han
21 Venetian Column
22 Mevlevi Tekke

Pages 78 and 79.

*Presidential Palace, Nicosia*

Museum ⑦ houses the island's most important collection of icons, dating from the 9th to 18th c.

The *Folk Art Museum* ⑧ is situated in the part of the old palace which is north of Ayios Ioannis. Peasant art and crafts featuring furniture, costumes, wood-carvings, hand-woven textiles, pottery, jewellery and commodities from all different periods are exhibited in 14 rooms of the former Benedictine monastery.

The *Struggle for Independence Museum* ⑨ provides a documented account of Cypriot resistance towards the British. It is located just to the north of the Folk Art Museum.

**Panayia Khrysaliniotissa** ⑩. When strolling through the old city do not forget to have a look at the *Khrysaliniotissa Church* situated on the corner of Odesseus Street and Arch. Philotheus Street. The oldest section was built in 1450 and houses a beautiful iconostasis.

**Hadji Georghakis Kornesios' House** ⑪ is the oldest remaining building from the Turkish period. It stands on Patriarch Gregorius Street and is a museum.

**Omerye Mosque** ⑫. Originally a 14th c. Christian church, it was converted to a mosque in 1571 by the Turkish conquerors of Nicosia. Sometimes it is possible to climb the minaret.

It would be a pity to leave the old city without having first wandered along *Ledra Street*; its many small boutiques make it the biggest shopping street. At *Eleftheria Square* you can appreciate for the last time the size and former importance of the city walls. These fortified walls surrounding the old city were built by the Venetians between 1567 and 1570. Several splendid buildings belonging to the much extended Nicosia of the Lusignan period were sacrificed for these defences. However, they were unable to prevent the Turkish conquest of the city. The 5-km-long system of fortified walls had eleven bastions and originally had three gates, Paphos Gate, Kyrenia Gate and Famagusta Gate. The heavy traffic coming into the city made further gaps in the wall necessary. A culture centre is housed in the impressive Famagusta Gate.

Many of the sights of the old city lie in the northern part (see page 77). Directly next to the Demarcation Line is the *Maronite Quarter* ⑬; the Maronites are members of a Lebanese church united with Rome.

**The Cyprus Museum** ⑭, located in Museum Street between Homer Avenue and Paphos Gate, is of international renown. You should allow at least three hours for visiting the collection, which is exhibited in 14 rooms.

*Room I:* contains exhibits from Neolithic and Chalcolithic sites, including Khirokitia, 5800–2300 B.C.

*Room II:* contains ceramics from the Early Bronze Age, 2300–1850 B.C.

*Room III:* traces the development of pottery in Cyprus from the Middle Bronze Age to the Roman period. Exhibits from the Bronze and Iron Ages, 1850–1000 B.C.

*Room IV:* Archaic terracotta figures from the temple at Ayia Irini.

*Room V:* features stone and marble statues from Archaic to Roman period. Outstanding is the marble statue of Aphrodite found at Soli, 1st c. B.C.

*Room VI:* contains statues from the Roman epoch, dominated by a large bronze statue of the Roman Emperor Septimus Severus, A.D. 193–211; famous sleeping Eros of Nea Paphos; bronze head of a boy from Soli, 2nd c. A.D.

*Room VII:* contains bronzes; helmets from Archaic and Hellenistic periods; portrait of Emperor Claudius; head of Zeus Ammon with eyes made of silver, 300–200 B.C.; new finds from tombs in Palea Paphos, 11th–8th c. B.C.; bowls on four wheels, 12th c. B.C.; outstanding collection of glassware from 14th c. B.C. to Roman period.

*Room VIII:* (Basement) contains the reconstructed tombs of different epochs, 3000–400 B.C.

*Room IX:* (Basement) Grave stelai and sarcophagi from different periods.

*Room X:* (Basement) Inscriptions on grave stelai; a horoscope from 1st c. A.D.

*Room XI:* (Upper Floor) Stately furniture from Tombs of the Kings at Salamis (Tomb 79), wooden bed and wooden throne inlaid with ivory, end of 8th c. B.C.; bronze kettle on an iron tripod decorated with eight griffins and four double-faced sirens (Tomb 79), end 8th c. B.C.; horses made from bronze, iron and ivory, bronze fittings from a wooden horse cart. Bronze statue of Horned God from Enkomi, 12th c. B.C.

*Room XII:* Reserved for temporary exhibitions and recent excavations.

*Room XIII:* Marble statues found at Salamis from Hellenistic and Roman periods, including Apollo playing the harp.

*Room XIV:* Terracotta figures from the Early Bronze Age to the Hellenistic period. Masks, votive statues. In the centre of the room are clay statues from Marion, 4th c. B.C.

Permission to take photographs must be obtained in writing.

⊗ *Date Club*, 2 Th. Dervis St.; *Ekali*, 1 St. Spyridon St.; *English Pub and Carvery*, 3 Pegasus St.

*Greek Tavern*, 46 Grivas Dhigenis Ave.; *Theos Tavern* (Cypriot), 59 Larnaca Rd.; *Grekos* (Cypriot), 3 Menandrou St.; *Kavouri* (Seafood), 125 Strovolos Ave.; *Psarolimano* (Fish), 142 Limassol Ave.; *Al Manar* (Arabic), 39 Th. Dervis St.; *Pagoda* (Chinese), 11 Louci Acrita Ave.

 *Africana*, 1 Michali Paridi St.; *Galaxy*, 44 I. Patatatsou St.; *Scorpios*, 3 Stasinos St.

 *Neraida*, Grivas Dhigenis Ave.; *Crazy Horse* (Cabaret), 186 Homer Ave.; *Elysee* (Bouzoukia - Greek dance music), Evagoras Ave.; *Fraktis* (Bouzoukia), Nicosia - Limassol Rd.

🛍 *Cypriot Handicrafts*, Athalassa Ave. and Laiki Yitonia. A shopping trip in Ledra St. in the old city and Makarios III St. in the new town is well worth while. Good buys include English cloth, made-to-measure suits, textiles, shoes, leather goods and jewellery.

🎪 *International Trade Fair* in May. Art festival in old city in September. Horse racing in Ayios Dhometios on Sundays.

ℹ *Cyprus Tourism Organisation'* Laiki Yitonia (east of Eleftherias Square). Tel. 02-444264 for information about:

🎸 🎭 🚗

✔ in Lapatsa (6 km).

## 🚌 Excursions from Nicosia

### Tamassos (22 km)

The region where Tamassos, one of the oldest towns on the island, once lay can be reached via Kato Lakatamia and Kato Dheftera on a good wide road. Even Homer made reference to the copper reserves of this town, the remains of which are now partly covered by the villages of Pera and Politiko. Two tombs (6th c. B.C.) were excavated in *Politiko* in 1890 by the German archaeologist Ohne-falsch-Richter. The architecture and decoration of the chambers in the rock indicate that important people lay buried here, probably the kings of Tamassos.

Not far from the village of Politiko lies the *Monastery of Heracleidios* which was built in its present form in 1759. St Heraclides was the first bishop of Tamassos and died a martyr.

🛍 Marzipan made by the nuns can be bought at the monastery (now a convent).

### Makheras Monastery Alt. 885 m (42 km)

Further on (past Kambia) along a winding, open road you come to the monastery of Makheras (Monastery of the Knife) at the foot of the 1420-m summit of Kionia. It was built by settlers in the 12th c., served as a refuge to the royal family during the plague in the 14th c., was burnt down in 1530 and 1892 and later rebuilt in the old style. From 1955–1959 it played a major role in the Cypriot struggle for independence. The resistance fighter Grigoris Afxendiou was burnt to death in a hiding place near the monastery.

✕ Souvla and Kleftiko are served in the monastery taverna.

### Perachorio Pop. 800 (17 km)

This village lies to the south of Nicosia on the road to Limassol. The Byzantine church *Ayii Apostoli*, situated on a small hill to the west, contains interesting wall paintings from the late 12th c. that have recently been restored.

### Peristerona Pop. 1200 (28 km)

This pretty village west of Nicosia, on the road to the spa resorts in the Troodos Mountains, contains a treasure that is featured on many a postcard of Cyprus — an imposing 11th c. *Byzantine church* with five cupolas, dedicated to St Barnabas and St Hilarion. Even if they have gone too far in restoring the interior, the 16th c. iconostasis is well worth seeing.

The 16th c. frescos in the church of *Ayia Barbara* lying to the west of the village are also of interest.

*St John's Cathedral, Nicosia*

# Larnaca and the South-East

The events of 1974 and the subsequent division of the island startled this sleepy corner of south-east Cyprus. The refugees from the North streamed into this region and a tremendous increase in economic prosperity followed. Larnaca and the surrounding area have at least partly taken over from Famagusta. New hotels outside the town's gates are indicative of a thriving tourist industry. The region of Ayia Napa and Paralimni, formerly disparagingly referred to as 'the potato corner' of the country, is well on the way to becoming a new holiday El Dorado. Here too frantic building activity is taking place, but fortunately the original character of the region has not been destroyed. The windmills still keep on turning in the sea breeze, pumping water on to the fertile fields. The red earth produces up to three vegetable and two potato crops a year.

The view across the gently undulating fields is occasionally broken up by citrus orchards and olive groves. The French poet Rimbaud spent some time here, fascinated by the incomparable light over land and sea and by the picturesque bays of the rugged coastline.

## Larnaca Pop. 40,000

Larnaca, capital of the province of the same name, lies on the south coast, just 50 km from Nicosia. Nowadays Jumbo-jets land at Larnaca Interna-

*Mosque, Larnaca*

tional Airport, only 10 km from the town centre, since Nicosia airport is only open to UN forces. Many ships which prior to 1974 used to head towards Famagusta, the busiest harbour on the island, now unload their cargo at Larnaca. Its industrial development is no less remarkable, yet despite refineries, factories and offices the old town has not lost the delightful charm of a provincial town with a past. The magnificent houses, the narrow busy streets and the promenade with its colonial buildings are the legacy of an era when several consulates and trading houses were to be found in the town.

###  History

The work of archaeologists has always been hampered by the building of the new town on top of the remains of the ancient site of *Kition*, founded in the 13th c. B.C. by the Mycenaeans. More recent excavations within the town have revealed that Kition itself was built on the remains of an even older settlement going back to the beginning of the 2nd millennium B.C.

This seems to endorse the prophets of the Old Testament, according to whom Noah's great-grandson Khettim is said to have taken over the island together with other lands after the flood, and to have founded a town in his own name which later became Kition.

Kition appears to have undergone a similar development to Alasia (see page 80). Evidence of destruction which was presumably caused by invading marauding pirates was found in one of the first Mycenaean strata of about 1400 B.C., from which large amounts of copper slack, clay pipes and melting pots were brought to light, as well as tombs containing valuable objects. In later years Kition's town centre was gradually to edge nearer the sea.

The whole island enjoyed the increased prosperity brought by the flourishing sea trade under the Phoenicians in the 8th c. B.C. Cyprus's greatest son, the philosopher Zeno, was born in 336 B.C., the time of Alexander the Great. A monument has been erected in the town park to this founder of Greek stoicism.

The new town originated after the Arab raids in the middle of the 7th c. A.D. It was moved about a mile inland in the Middle Ages to the district where the Bishop of Kition's residence still stands today. Under the Turks (1573–1878) Larnaca boomed as Cyprus's chief harbour and the base of the main trading and shipping companies, until Famagusta extended its harbour and soon overtook Kition.

📷 **Sightseeing**

**St Lazarus Church** ①. This triple-naved church was built in the 9th c. by Emperor Leo the Philosopher. In 890 a tomb was discovered on this site which was believed to be that of Lazarus whom Christ brought back to life. According to legend he was the first bishop of the town. The saint's coffin is preserved beneath the chancel. His remains, which were plundered during the Crusades, are in Marseilles.

The church, which stands in the old business quarter, has been extended several times. It was a rare privilege under the Turkish rule to be allowed to

erect the free-standing church tower. The iconostasis dates from the 18th c.

**Larnaca Fort** ② was built in its present form in 1625 by the Turks, assimilating the older Venetian fortifications. Today it houses a small museum which contains information on the origin of Kition and the excavations at Hala Sultan Tekke.

In the **Regional Archaeological Museum** ③ on Kalogreon Square there are two rooms containing exhibits from Neolithic times to the Middle Ages.

*Room I:* contains finds from Khirokitia, Mycenaean bowls and vases from Pyla, the first geometric pots from Kition, cylindrical stamps from the Bronze Age, Roman glassware, jewellery from the late Bronze Age up to the beginning of the 1st c. A.D. and pottery from the Middle Ages.

*Room II:* contains sculptures from Arsos and Kition, terracotta statues and grave stelai.

**Excavations** ④, ⑤. The earlier Acropolis of Kition lies directly north of the Regional Museum. The so-called Damboula Hill was levelled by the British in the last century.

The most interesting of the

*Above: Walking in the cloisters of the church of St Lazarus.*
*Left: Icon screen in St Lazarus church.*

excavations I-IV of old Kition is Area II
which can be found to the north of Archbishop Kyprianou Avenue. The remains of a temple complex discovered here originate from the 13th c. B.C.

**Pierides Collection** ⑥ at 4 Zenon Kitieus Street (Swedish Consulate). This should not be missed. It was begun last century by honorary consul Demetrios Pierides and is a unique private collection of Cypriot antiquities. There are four rooms containing outstanding discoveries from the Neolithic to the Roman period.

 *Alakati* and *Dyonisos*, Ankara St., near the fort. Other tavernas and cafés are on the seafront (Athens St.).

 In the main hotels.

🎵 *Pussy Cat*, Makarios Ave.; *Spilia*, 28 Zenon Pierides St.

🍷 *Golden Night* (Cabaret), 25 Galileos St.; *Nostalgia* (Bouzoukia), 57 General Timayia St.

*Larnaca Tourist Beach*, 8 km east towards Dhekelia, has every amenity including a restaurant.

*Kataklysmos*, celebrated 50 days after Easter, at Whitsuntide. This Greek Orthodox water festival is well and truly celebrated at Larnaca. On the Saturday before Palm Sunday the icon of St Lazarus is carried through the streets in a procession to mark the Saint's Day.

*Cypriot Handicrafts* is situated at 6 Cosma Lysioti St.; Zenon Kitieus St. is best for shopping.

Ⓐ *Forest Beach Camping*, east of Larnaca; tel. 041-22414 .

ℹ️ *Cyprus Tourism Organisation*, Democratias Sq., tel. 041-54322; and at Larnaca airport, tel. 041-54389.

Brochures are available at the yacht harbour, Larnaca Marina, with information on:

## 🚌 Excursions from Larnaca

### Pyla (6 km)
Pyla is situated in the UN-controlled buffer zone between the two parts of the island. Both Greek and Turkish Cypriots still live together in this village. There are Greek and Turkish schools, Greek and Turkish shops, many Greek restaurants and also a Turkish café in the village square.

### Salt Lake (5 km)
South of Larnaca, directly by the airport, lies one of Cyprus's two salt lakes. The bottom of this 6 sq. km lake

*Tekke Mosque*

is 2–3 m below sea level. In August, when the water has evaporated, a 5–10 cm salt crust forms; the salt has been collected since ancient times. During the time of the Lusignans Larnaca was referred to as *Salina* due to the annual collection of 3500 tons of salt.

In winter, when it has filled with rainwater, the lake is a favourite stopping place for migrating birds, particularly flamingos.

Legend has it that the lake owes its existence to St Lazarus, who at the time when the lake was still covered with vineyards passed by, desperate with thirst and hunger, and asked the owner to give him a few grapes. The miserly woman lied and said, 'Stranger, my vines have withered this year and have not produced a single grape.' Lazarus retorted, 'Because you have lied to me your vineyard shall dry up and become a salt lake,' and so it did.

**Hala Sultan Tekke.** On the banks of the

Salt Lake there is an oasis with palms and cypress trees in the centre of which stands a mosque. The minaret towering out of this seemingly exotic spot is visible from afar and belongs to Hala Sultan Tekke, one of the holiest places of Islam. Even at the time of Turkish rule all visiting ships of the Ottoman Empire had to lower their flag as a mark of respect, for the Tekke contains the tomb of Umm Haram, one of Mohammed's aunts. According to tradition Umm Haram is said to have fallen off her donkey while accompanying the Arab invaders in A.D. 647, breaking her 'alabaster neck' in the process and so giving up her 'victorious spirit'. The present tomb was built in 1760 and the mosque in 1816.

### Panayia Angeloktistos in Kiti.

Just 6 km south of the Salt Lake is the village of *Kiti*. The church of Panayia Angeloktistos, 'built by the angels', is an impressive construction from the 10th c. with an addition from the Lusignan period. The mosaic in the apse which was uncovered in 1952 indicates the existence of an older church. The Byzantine mosaic, which could be 6th c., is exceptional. The Virgin Mary is represented with the Christ child on her arm, his right hand raised in blessing. She is approached by Archangels Michael (left, damaged) and Gabriel, both carrying a sceptre and an orb, each with a cross on top. Their wings are of peacock feathers.

### Stavrovouni Monastery Alt. 690 m (30 km)

The Stavrovouni Monastery (Mount of the Holy Cross) stands on the most easterly peak of the Troodos Mountains. It can be seen from many miles away. St Helena, the mother of Emperor Constantine, is said to have founded this monastery, the oldest in Cyprus, in A.D. 327. Prior to this time Aphrodite was worshipped on this very spot. Nowadays the faithful worship a relic from the cross

of Christ and the cross of the Repentant Sinner. The founder of the monastery brought both relics with her from Judaea and so made Stavrovouni into the most important place of pilgrimage on the island.

The walls of this monastery building, which was designed along the lines of a fortress, were, in their present form, built mainly in the 19th c. About 15 monks still live in the monastery, their water supply being stored in four

cisterns; they will gladly offer the thirsty pilgrim some refreshment. Women are only admitted on a Sunday. A platform behind the apse of the church provides an unforgettable view encompassing Larnaca and the bay.

## Pyrga Pop. 260 (20 km)

The traveller who passes through Pyrga, which nestles in the olive groves along the minor road from Larnaca to the main Nicosia—Limassol highway,

will not regret stopping for a while. After refreshment in the café on the village square you can ask for the key to the *Royal Chapel of St Catherine* which is just a few yards away.

The church was probably built in 1421 by the Roman Catholic King Janus, who had it painted by an indigenous Orthodox artist. Consequently the frescos are in the Byzantine style but contain some western elements, for example

*Panayia Angeloktistos*

*Stavrovouni Monastery*

inscriptions in medieval French. One of the wall paintings, which unfortunately are not in particularly good condition, depicts Janus with his wife Queen Charlotte at the foot of a crucifixion scene which is only partially preserved. Other scenes include 'The Last Supper', 'The Raising of Lazarus', 'Christ's Procession into Jerusalem' and 'The Death of Mary'.

## Lefkara Alt. 585 m; Pop. 2100 (39 km)

Pano Lefkara lies west of Larnaca. As you approach, the view of the twin villages of Upper (Pano) Lefkara and Lower (Kato) Lefkara, with their Mediterranean charm, is quite beautiful. The azure-blue and white houses with red roofs perch on a gently

*Stavrovouni Monastery*

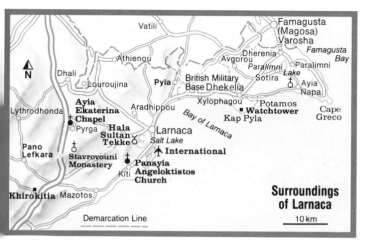

descending slope surrounded by almond, apricot, fig and olive trees. The courtyards, loggias and terraces bustle with activity.

Lefkara owes its prosperity and far-reaching fame to its women. Leonardo da Vinci is said to have purchased Lefkara lace here in 1481 for furnishing Milan Cathedral. The art of lace-making and embroidery was passed on from generation to generation and the visitor can hardly fail to be impressed by the symmetry of the geometric pattern. However, do remember to haggle, as prices actually tend to be lower in the towns! But Lefkara has even more to offer — fine gold and silver work and okoum, a sweet which used to be made by the Turkish Cypriots when they lived here.

## Khirokitia (30 km)

Apart from Kalavassos-Tenta this is the oldest settlement discovered so far in Cyprus; it is of Stone Age origin — about 7000 B.C. It is situated west of Larnaca.

Of the original 1000 stone huts 61 have been excavated to date. The round buildings covered with beehive like domed roofs and with walls 2–3 m thick were built so close together and so compact that their occupants must have felt like mussels in a shell. Other more spacious dwellings have been found, indicating that within the village

*Craftwork, Lefkara*

population estimated at 2000–3000 there was a significant social divide. The contents of the graves discovered in the big tholoi were richer and more precious than those in the more humble round dwellings. The fact that female graves were without exception more luxuriously equipped than those of males is due to the special status that women enjoyed under the domination of the 'Great Mother'. The odd thing about Khirokitia is that its occupants actually lived over their dead — the deceased members of the family stayed in the house; they just moved downstairs below the floor of the hut. Under one house the skeletons of 26 adults and children were found at eight different levels.

Among the contents of the graves were idols to a presumably female goddess, artistic stone vessels, pearl jewellery, shells and amulets in the shape of clubs and axes. Beside these artefacts were found some stone arrowheads together with the bones of the animals killed by them — red deer, ibex and moufflon. The finds from the graves are on permanent display in the Cyprus Museum in Nicosia.

## Ayia Napa Pop. 2000

There are two routes to reach Ayia Napa from Larnaca; both involve crossing the sovereign British military base Dhekelia. The most interesting road leads through Xylotymbou and the UN-controlled buffer zone via *Dherinia* (the hospital has a good view of Famagusta). The shorter road runs along the coast through the potato-growing centre Xylophagou.

Until 1974 Ayia Napa was only a fishing village with no more than ten houses. Since the Turkish invasion it has become a modern, well kept holiday resort with more than 7000 hotel beds.

### 📷 Monastery of Ayia Napa

The medieval monastery of Ayia Napa can be found towards the coast on the outskirts of the old village centre with its numerous tavernas and cafés. The recently renovated buildings date from about 1500.

As is often the case there is a legend attached to its origins: a hunter followed the sound of his dog's insistent barking to a cave in the forest. In the cave he found a miraculously illuminated icon of the Virgin Mary. (This has a historical explanation. At the time of Byzantine iconoclasm (8th–9th c.) icons were often taken to a safe place.) News of the discovery quickly spread among the pious in the region. A young jilted Venetian noblewoman got to hear of this holy place where pilgrims soon built a chapel. The young woman decided to retreat there and had a monastery, an olive press and a mil built. As she was a Catholic she also

*The beach at Ayia Napa*

*Ayia Napa Monastery*

had a second chapel built. Even the mighty mulberry-fig trees outside the walls, which advertise the monastery from afar, are said to have been planted by her.

The cloister, which seems to radiate peace and well-being, has arcades providing shade on three sides. It is reached by a two-storey gateway. At the southern end water splashes from a marble boar's head, probably of 16th c. origin but which has also been attributed to the Romans. The water in the octagonal marble fountain basin, below the cupola of the open-sided fountain-house in the centre of the courtyard, also provides a cooling effect. The decorative garlands and statues, including those of the founder and her parents, are worth seeing.

The monastery church has an unusual doorway partly hewn out of the cliff. There is a Catholic chapel just to the east. Nowadays the rooms of the monastery are used for ecumenical meetings.

*In the dunes at Nissi Beach*

## A special tip

It is marvellous to go out to sea with the fishermen early in the morning, to watch them fishing and experience the dawn. Enquire in the fish restaurants at the harbour.

 Ideal holiday resort; many lovely beaches, hotels and apartments.

 *Nissi Beach* (Hotel), *Sandy Bay, Golden Sands* (2–3 km west from Ayia Napa harbour) and *Ayia Napa Beach* (to the east) are fine sandy beaches. They slope gently into the clear water. An ideal playground for children. Those wishing to stay all day by the sea can hire deck chairs and sunshades, take a shower and eat in the beach taverna. All beaches have:

*Nissi Beach* and *Grecian Bay Hotel:*

 *Napa Tavern, Stone Garden, Magic Sandy Bay* and *Psarolimano* (last two specialise in fish).

 *Nissi Disco* (in Nissi Beach Hotel), *Cave Disco, Aquarium.*

 *Grecian Bay Hotel.*

 *Cyprus Tourism Organisation;* tel: 037–21796.

## Excursions from Ayia Napa

The varied coastline of south-east Cyprus offers picturesque places to visit.

### Cape Pyla

*Potamos* (8 km west of Ayia Napa) is a sleepy cove where a handful of brightly coloured fishing boats await the dawn. If you do not feel like walking the 2 km to the ruins of a Venetian watch tower at Cape Pyla, there is an inviting taverna instead. Potamos, meaning 'river', lies on a stream which only flows for a few months of the year.

### Cape Greco and the East Coast

Experienced walkers wearing stout footwear can explore the countryside and rocky coast as far as Cape Greco (5 km) while enjoying the fresh sea breeze; it can also be reached by car. Access to the south-eastern tip of the island is forbidden. A British radar station and a radio transmitter belonging to Radio Monte Carlo are cordonned off by a high fence.

### Fig Tree Bay 5 km north of Cape Greco

The crystal-clear water is perfect for water sports. A beach taverna proudly claims to own the original fig tree on the island, brought by invaders from the east in the 17th c. according to the sign.

### Paralimni

The hotels which lie to the north of Fig Tree Bay directly on the seafront actually belong to Paralimni. The same leisure and sporting facilities are available here. Paralimni itself lies 5 km past these hotels. Travelling by the direct road across country it is only 4 km from Ayia Napa. There are no particular tourist attractions here, just good food on offer in the tavernas.

At the northern end of *Dhereni* (3 km north of Paralimni) the visitor comes across the stark political reality of the Green Line — sandbags, barbed wire and watchtowers. If it was not there it would only take ten minutes to reach Famagusta. Instead the visitor can see the ghost town of *Varosha.* former stronghold of tourism, Varosha is now prohibited to both Turkish and Greek Cypriots. To the north, in the distance, you can make out the Karpas peninsula at the end of the Bay of Famagusta, which today is part of the Turkish zone.

# Limassol Pop. 110,000

Limassol, the second largest town on Cyprus, lies on the south coast of the island. The number of ships at anchor in Akrotiri Bay is indicative of the harbour's importance. It used to be the main export harbour but since 1974 it has become the principal port in Cyprus. The population has almost doubled since 1974 as the region had to absorb 43,000 refugees.

Formerly a commercial, industrial and administrative centre, Limassol is becoming increasingly important for tourism. A chain of newly built hotels and holiday developments stretches east along the coast as far as Amathus. This is doubtless due to the central position Limassol enjoys: 72 km from Paphos, 64 km from Larnaca, 81 km from Nicosia and only 54 km from the Troodos Mountains. It is ideally situated for the holidaymaker who wishes to visit the country's sights.

The people of Limassol are sociable and easy-going. Their festivals are famous throughout the country; the exuberance of the Carnival in spring and the frivolity of the Wine Festival in autumn attract many visitors. Limassol is the centre of the Cypriot wine industry. Other important industries based in Limassol are oil refineries, lemonade factories, carob processing and fruit canning. Although Limassol has little in the way of history, it is a very attractive up-to-date town with a boulevard of modern shops that crosses the new town. Towards the sea there is the old town with its narrow streets and typically Cypriot tavernas, and along the sea front which stretches for miles cafés, sports clubs, nightspots, hotels of various categories, a park and even a zoo are to be found interspersed among the tall eucalyptus trees and flower gardens. There is much variety in the surrounding countryside, and for the tourist interested in art history there are some rewarding places to visit.

 ## History

Just because there is only one historical monument for the tourist to visit — the castle dating in its present form from the 14th c.— this does not mean that Limassol is without history. Indeed, this town can be traced back to the 2nd millennium B.C. However, the settlement cannot have been of great importance for a long time, as it was not until the 5th c. A.D. that it was granted the status of a town by the Emperor Theodosius II, and named Theodosias after him. 200 years later Theodosias fell victim to the Arab raids. The survivors fled to ancient Amathus, which was 8 km to the east, and which was destroyed in A.D. 1191 by Richard the Lionheart. After this blow the descendants of the refugees returned to their home town with the Amathusians who had also been made homeless. They rebuilt Theodosias but the town continued to attract misfortune — it was plundered and burnt down by the Genoese in 1373, by the Mameluks in 1426 and again by the Turks in 1570. In 1584 it was destroyed by an earthquake. In 1815 Limassol was a village with a population of 150.

 ## Sightseeing

**The Castle.** The present castle which originated in the 14th c. stands in the centre of the old Turkish quarter. In the chapel of its Byzantine predecessor Richard the Lionheart is said to have married Princess Berengaria. The fortifications were able to withstand, for the most part, the devastating earthquake of 1584 after they had become Turkish bulwarks in 1570. During the period of British rule it served as a prison. Nowadays it houses a museum of medieval town history. From the castle roof there is a beautiful view of the town, port and sea.

---

**A special tip**

You should visit one of the big wine-presses, or rather wine factories, in Limassol in order to find out about and taste the Cypriot wines, liqueurs and brandies. The tours are in the mornings. Ask at your hotel or at the CTO.

---

**Archaeological Museum.** This newly opened museum in Byron St. is well worth a visit.

*Room I* (on the left): contains stone axes from the Neolithic and Chalcolithic periods, an outstanding collection of Cypro-geometric and Archaic ceramics, and artefacts excavated at Amathus and Curium.

*Room II*: terracotta statues, gold jewellery 17th c. B.C.—4th c. A.D., glassware from the Cypro-archaic to the Roman period, extensive coin collections from the Limassol region, new finds from Amathus.

*Room III*: Two columns from Amathus, 6th c. B.C.; statues of the Egyptian god Bes; marble head of Aphrodite from Curium, 4th c. B.C.; grave stelai; lower part of a male marble statue with crossed legs, from Amathus, Hellenistic period; head of a bearded man from Phassoula, 4th c. A.D.; marble table from the Temple of Apollo at Curium.

**Market halls.** They are the most oriental and the liveliest in the whole of Cyprus. They are situated in the heart of the old town.

⚔ *Avenida Limassol*, Limassol-Nicosia Road; *Avenida Famagusta*, 6 Marconi St.; *Camaro*, 230 Makarios Ave.; *Neon Faliron* (Fish), 135 Gladstone St.

⊗ *Panku* (Chinese), Limassol-Nicosia Rd.; *Scotis Steak House*, corner of Makarios and Souli St.

*Limassol, fishing harbour*

♫ *Caribbean* and *Trans Disco*, both on Limassol-Nicosia Rd.; *Triangle*, Potamos Yermasoyias.

⊻ *Le Panache*, 86 Makarios Ave.; *Archontissa*, Makarios Ave.; *Brittania*, Fr. Roosevelt Ave.; all have Bouzoukia (Greek dance music).

⌂ *Dhasoudi Beach* (5 km to the east) has changing rooms, a restaurant and water sports. At the big hotels on the Limassol-Nicosia road there are:

⌂ *Cypriot Handicrafts*, 25 Themidos St.; St Andreas St. is an interesting shopping area.

February or March: the *Limassol Carnival* lasting 10 days. There is a masked ball and a procession with decorated floats.

July/August: the International Folk Festival attracts dance troupes in national costumes from all over the world.

September: the Wine Festival with folk dancing, folk music and free wine-tasting.

*Cyprus Tourism Organisation*, 15 Spyrou Araouzos St.; tel: 051 62756 for information on:

## Excursions from Limassol

### Amathus (8 km)

There is not a great deal of ancient Amathus, east of Limassol, left to see. Sheep graze on the excavated tombs of the necropolis and there is nothing left of the Temple of Aphrodite, lauded by Catullus and Virgil. The acropolis once stood at the point where the Limassol-Nicosia Road curves to the left along the coast, about 100 m east of the Amathus Beach Hotel which is built on the site of a necropolis. It might have been crowned by the aforesaid temple. Found here were a stone vase of 3.2 m diameter (in 1866) and recently the stone torso of a female figure wearing a necklace. The ruins of the old city wall surrounding the acropolis are clearly visible. Within the enclosure of the lower city of Amathus, facing inland from the sea (toward Ayios Thykonas), and at the end of the eastern necropolis (near Ayia Varvara), two early Christian basilicas (6th—7th c.) were discovered. Excavations in the lower city exposed the 6th c. columns now in the Limassol Museum. The harbour and parts of the town are today covered by the sea.

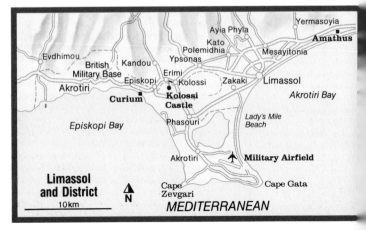 Amathus, capital of one of the nine ancient kingdoms of Cyprus, was the only city that stubbornly resisted the Greek colonisation of around 1000 B.C. Numerous legends and myths tell of the pride with which the Amathusians defended their land and identity. They sought to keep their religious beliefs — they still worshipped Aphrodite in her primitive form, as in Asia Minor, as a mother goddess who embodied both male and female roles. This is known from a statue of Aphrodite Amathusia which portrays her as a bearded hermaphrodite in female clothing holding a sceptre, and also from the ritual exchanging of clothes as practised by the priests and priestesses at the shrine of Amathus, and which symbolised dual sexuality.

In classical times Amathus was famous for its numerous temples dedicated to the Olympian gods. After the Arab raids in the 7th c. A.D. the inner part of the city was fortified and given the title *Kastro* (castle). The end came for Amathus when the English king Richard the Lionheart landed in A.D. 1191 — first he laid siege to it and then he destroyed it. The city never recovered from this blow. The survivors packed their worldly goods and moved to Theodosias 8km to the west, from which Limassol developed.

## Kalavassos-Tenta

Round houses from the middle of the 8th millennium were discovered in Kalavassos-Tenta, between the excavated sites of Amathus and Khirokitia. Inside one of them a wall painting was found depicting a human figure with raised arms. The excavations are still in progress.

## Akrotiri Peninsula

On the peninsula lies the British army base of the same name. Only the strip of land south of the village of *Akrotiri* is a restricted zone. The countryside of the peninsula is one of contrast. There are almost endless citrus plantations, and countless vines on which ripen the grapes that make the sweet wine Commandaria. Footpaths leading through the luxurious vegetation frequently become overgrown with greenery.

Then there is a *Salt Lake* here, dried up and desolate in summer. In winter the picture is quite different when the flamingos and migrating birds arrive and fill the area with life.

### Lady's Mile Beach

This beautiful stretch of sandy beach lies on the east coast with views of Limassol and the Troodos Mountains. It gets very busy here at weekends.

### Kolossi Castle (11 km)

Kolossi Castle, 11 km west of Limassol, was the seat first of the Templars and then of the Knights of St John in the Lusignan period (1192–1489). Both orders, originally established for the protection and welfare of Christian pilgrims in the Holy Land, had ensured their own safety by acquiring extensive areas of land in Cyprus, when defeat started to become obvious in the Holy Land itself and the end of the Crusades could be foreseen. The Templars, especially, commanded enormous wealth when they settled on Cyprus. However, both their riches and their retreat, the ancient island of Aphrodite, were to be their downfall. Pope Clement and King Philip of France planned a crusade which, as soon became clear, was aimed less at the Holy Land than at the wealth of the Templars. Moreover, Philip had all the Templars in his territory arrested and taken to court in Paris where in 1309 they were condemned as heretics and burnt to death in large numbers. They were charged with worshipping pagan idols, possibly a reference to the mysterious black stone from the shrine of Aphrodite which at that time was still situated in Paphos, not far from the

*Kolossi Castle*

castle of the Knights Templar. While the wealth of the Templars was shrinking, the members of the order were being systematically tortured and the Great Master was burnt at the stake in 1314 in Paris. The Knights of St John were already installed in the former seat of the Templars' power at Kolossi. Their stay in Cyprus was prosperous but no less troubled. The Knights never relinquished their command base at Kolossi, even during their dominion of Rhodes. They cultivated sugar cane, maize and olives. The ruins of a sugar factory and remains of a mill are directly adjacent to the castle. That the Knights have literally remained 'on everybody's lips' in Cyprus until the present day is due to the finest product of their agriculture — the sweet wine Commandaria, which is named after them and is the best known of all Cypriot wines today.

The castle, as it stands today, was built in 1454 by the Knights of the Order of St John. It stands 25 m high with its well preserved walls almost 3 m thick. The basic square shape is repeated from the basement to the third floor, sometimes being divided into two rooms. The view from the roof over the whole of the surrounding area justifies the climb.

### Episkopi Pop. 2000

3 km to the west of Kolossi at Erimi the road crosses the River Kouris which dries up in summer. Should you wish to visit the *Curium Museum* in the village of Episkopi turn right immediately past the bridge and follow the signposts. Exhibits from Curium, Erimi, Bamboula and Kaloriziki are displayed in a charming cottage. It is a worthwhile stop for the visitor interested in Curium.

### Curium

From Episkopi to Curium (Gk. *Kourion)* is 2 km. The region of Curium was already populated in the Stone Age. Achaean settlers came with the first wave of Mycenaean colonisation in the 14th c. B.C., followed by further Greek settlers in the 12th c. B.C. This is reinforced by the accounts of Herodotus, who maintained that Curium was an establishment of settlers from Argos. Situated on the steep coast west of the rebuilt village of Episkopi, Curium was one of the nine kingdoms at the time of the kings in the 7th c. B.C.

Under Ptolemaic and Roman rule Curium was a town of considerable importance. Although it was badly damaged in the earthquakes of A.D. 332 and 342, it was rebuilt and flourished until the middle of the 7th c. A.D., when the Arab raids and further natural disasters finally destroyed the town. The first excavations began in 1873.

### Sightseeing

**Achilles Mosaic.** The building which houses the *Achilles Mosaic*, formerly close to Paphos Gate, is on the main Limassol—Paphos road. There were once rooms grouped around what today are the remains of an open courtyard, and a covered walkway protected a beautiful mosaic floor of the 4th c. A.D. The mosaic shows a scene from the court of King Lykomedes. Achilles, disguised as a maiden, is quickly recognised by the cunning Odysseus who is then able to take him to fight in the Trojan Wars. Achilles is shown clutching a spear and shield behind the gift he is offering, as if it were the natural thing to do.

**House of the Gladiators.** The floors of two rooms of a former villa are

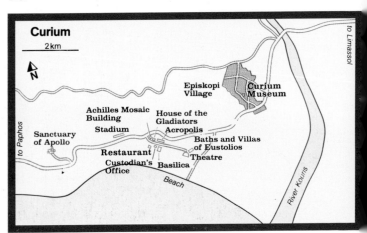

*Curium*

*Curium Theatre*

decorated with gladiatorial scenes. The colours of the mosaics have been exceptionally well preserved.

**Acropolis.** Opposite the custodian's office is the acropolis of Curium which was destroyed by an earthquake in the 4th c. A.D. It has been uncovered since the middle of the 1970s. From here you can also get to the aforementioned mosaics. Several Corinthian columns have been re-erected in their former positions.

**Basilica.** Judging from the style of the capitals it was built in the 5th c. A.D. as a cathedral for the bishops of Curium. The nave was separated from the aisles by 12 granite columns on each side. The single apse was flanked by right-angled rooms which were concealed from the aisles by pairs of columns. Paved walkways outside led past the aisles. A paved forecourt with a hexagonal fountain was situated in front of the spacious narthex (ante-nave), which adjoins a partly excavated baptistry with a mosaic floor. The façade of the church enjoys a magnificent view of the rugged steep cliffs of the coastline and the beach far below.

**Theatre.** It held around 3500 spectators. The seats around the semi-circular orchestra are reached via a barrel-vaulted passage with five entrances. The fly-tower was originally on a level with the highest seats. The theatre was in use from the 2nd c. B.C. to the 4th c. A.D., including a short period of misuse for animal baiting in the 3rd c. A.D.

---

### A special tip

A theatrical performance or concert in the classical theatre at Curium (or Paphos) is an unforgettable experience, and you can test the outstanding acoustics of these theatres for yourself. Classical Greek dramas and also Shakespearian plays are performed in the summer months. Enquire at your hotel reception or at the CTO.

---

**Baths and Villas of Eustolios.** East of the theatre and adjoining its stair tower extend the walls of a palatial building from the 5th c. A.D. It may have been some sort of public bathing establishment as it was equipped with an extensive and comfortable bath-house. A fragmented mosaic inscription (in the East Wing) mentions the founder Eustolios, 'this cool refuge sheltered from the wind', and Apollo, the protector of heathen Curium. In contrast another inscription mentions Christ. The show-piece of the site is a remarkably preserved mosaic floor in the central room (north part). It features a strikingly beautiful young woman who personifies creation (Ktisis). In her right hand she is holding a measure which is actually the same length as a Roman foot. No less fascinating is the panel of mosaic depicting a partridge surrounded by birds and fishes. Sunken foot baths connect the central room with the cold baths, while to the west can be seen the warm air chambers which served to heat the baths.

**Stadium.** The stadium, built in the 2nd c. A.D., lies about 1 km to the west of the Acropolis on the edge of the town. It was in use up to A.D. 400. Only the U-shaped outline with three gateways remains from this vast enclosure which seated 6000 spectators. Part of the seating has been reconstructed.

**Sanctuary of Apollo.** A mile further west lies the Sanctuary of Apollo Hylates. Evidently as early as the 8th c. B.C. Apollo the god of the forests was worshipped here, one of the most sacred sites of ancient Cyprus, and at one time it was enclosed in a game reserve. The ruins that exist today are mostly part of a temple constructed much later, about A.D. 100. It was probably badly damaged by the earthquake in the 4th c., but remained in use until the 5th c. As is usual in

*Mosaic floor at Curium*

*Sunset at Curium*

Cyprus the (rebuilt) temple is a relatively small building as the rituals were normally held outside. A wide flight of steps and a vestibule with four chambers led to the altar. According to Strabo (Greek geographer and historian at the beginning of the 1st c. A.D.) whoever touched the altar paid with his life without fail — he would be thrown into the sea.

The buildings in the best condition are the ancient pilgrim hostels and Roman baths. Archaeologically the most significant find is a circular monument from pre-Christian times with a diameter of 18 m. It was excavated between 1978 and 1980 and is now fenced off. In the unusual round hollows may have stood the young trees consecrated to Apollo around which the pilgrims carried out sacred dances or processions. Nothing like it has yet been discovered in the whole of the Mediterranean area.

# Paphos Pop. 21,000

Paphos, the name used today to refer to the twin towns of Ktima and Nea (New) Paphos, is situated 153 km from Nicosia and 136 km from Larnaca on Cyprus's south-west coast. The climate here is the mildest on the island.

Increasing numbers of tourists are expected to visit the town and region of Paphos, understandably attracted by its many beaches and historic sights and the opportunity to explore the west of the island in peace. Since 1983 Paphos has had its own airport.

Industry, too, has expanded since 1974. Greek Cypriot refugees from the north have taken the place of the Turkish Cypriots who earlier constituted a third of the population.

## Ktima

This part of the town is the seat of local government and of the Bishop of Paphos. Ktima lies 3 km inland from Nea Paphos on a rocky plateau 45 m above sea level. Ktima is a traditional agricultural centre and its population makes a reasonable living from the huge banana and almond plantations, the biggest on the island.

where the inhabitants of Nea Paphos sought refuge after the Arab raids in the 7th c. In 1540 the population was about 2000. Nowadays this small town owes its charm and pride to the numerous neo-classical buildings erected during the period of British colonial rule. Not until the mid 19th c. did Ktima develop into a prosperous and proud provincial town.

 ## History

Evidence of Stone Age and Mycenaean settlements has been discovered in Ktima. It might have been the place

 ## Sightseeing

In Ktima the exteriors of the classical buildings of 19th c. origin are of interest — *three gymnasia* ①,* the *town hall* ②,

* Refer to map on page 63

*Paphos Harbour*

and the *Kebir Mosque* ③. The town has three interesting museums.

The *Archaeological Museum* ④ contains finds from the early Stone Age to the Middle Ages in its three rooms. The collection of Roman clay hot water bottles in the shapes of parts of the body is unique.

The *Byzantine Museum* ⑤ has numerous beautiful icons from the post-Byzantine era (15th—19th c.) as well as liturgical objects and garments.

The *Ethnographical Museum* ⑥ contains the private collection of Prof. Eliades — a cross-section of rural folk culture.

**Nea Paphos** This part of the town, sometimes referred to as Kato (Lower) Paphos, lies below Ktima directly on the coast.

## 🐚 History

Architectural ruins abound in this charming garden town, the history of which, according to legend, stretches back to the Mycenaean period (1400 B.C.). Yet in the first centuries of its existence Nea Paphos only seems to have served as a harbour for the pilgrims heading for the Temple of Aphrodite at Old Paphos, 12 km to the east. They walked from here to the temple in a festive procession wearing garlands of flowers and accompanied by music.

The history of Nea Paphos became more eventful towards the end of the 4th c. B.C. with the beginning of the rule of the Egyptian Ptolemies, who in the 2nd c. B.C. expanded it into the chief military base and naval station. This enabled the town to retain a certain amount of independence which benefited its cultural and economic development.

The most glorious epoch in the history of Nea Paphos began when Cyprus was conquered by the Romans in 58 B.C. It became the new island capital and one of the first Roman governors was Cicero (51—50 B.C.), for whom the development of the town was so important that he expressly required his successor to take responsibility for it. Nea Paphos became an elegant city of metropolitan splendour. Even a severe earthquake in the reign of Augustus could not destroy it. The rebuilding programme supported at the highest imperial level was so successful that Strabo (63 B.C.—A.D.20) was able to write about a 'flourishing town surrounded by mighty walls with a magnificent temple and public buildings'.

Following its successful conversion to Christianity Nea Paphos is said to have had 365 Christian churches so that mass could be celebrated in a different church every day. The decline of Nea Paphos began with a series of earthquakes in the 4th c. A.D. which devastated large parts of the town. The earthquakes were followed by the Arabs, whose first attack caused the Byzantines to build a powerful fortress close to the port. This first attack was followed by a further 24, primarily in search of the treasures protected in the churches. Following its decline the town enjoyed a period of modest prosperity under the Lusignans. However, the riches bestowed upon the town by the Franks, the *Frankish Baths* and *Frankish Cathedral* of which only the ruins remain today, were destroyed together with Nea Paphos by a further earthquake in A.D. 1222. A large part of its population moved to present-day Ktima and those who stayed behind united in a close village community whose descendants today fill the ruins of the old town with life.

## 📷 Sightseeing

The so-called **Tombs of the Kings** ⑦ originate from the 3rd c. B.C. There are over 100 luxurious mock houses for the dead of wealthy families; they consist of

*Paphos — Tombs of the Kings*

a courtyard, which is in part surrounded by an elegant portico of Doric columns, and of burial chambers hewn even deeper out of the rock in which the dead rested as if in sleeping chambers. They probably represent an Alexandrian style of tomb and they are the only monuments from the Hellenistic period in Cyprus.

## The Catacombs of St Solomoni ⑤
consist of several underground chambers which may never have been used as tombs. They presumably acted as places of refuge in early Christian times. During the Byzantine period a room was extended into a chapel and in the 12th c. it was decorated with

frescos. Unfortunately these are in a poor state of repair and to have a closer look you will need to locate the light switch just past the first step on the right. According to tradition St Solomoni, mother of the seven Maccabees, was tortured to death with her seven children in 168 B.C. Solomoni is described as a saint although she lived before the birth of Christ. This is because the Eastern Church did not have an institutionalised process of canonisation, and the designation 'saint' can also be established on the basis of local tradition. The many prayer cloths tied to the boughs of the turpentine-pistachio tree overshadowing the entrance are

*Ganymede and the Eagle, Paphos mosaic*

*House of Dionysos, Paphos*

dedicated to St Solomoni and this shows that the chapel is still in use.

**Latin Cathedral** ⑨. Only the tower-like south-west corner remains of this probably Gothic 14th c. cathedral, built as the see of a bishop.

**Acropolis, Odeon, Agora, Asklepeion** ⑩. The Roman *Odeon* lies at the base of a modern lighthouse standing on the rocks of the *Acropolis* of Nea Paphos. The partly restored semicircular theatre has an auditorium of 12 rows, an orchestra and a stage hewn out of the rock. The 2nd c. Odeon was part of a building complex to which belonged the *Agora* (market and square) adjoining the east side and the *Asklepeion* lying to the south (shrine and healing centre of god of healing, Asklepeios).

**House of Dionysos** ⑪, formerly a 22-roomed Roman villa, is where every visitor to Paphos heads for. In 14 of the rooms adjoining the atrium exceptionally colourful and expressive mosaics in good condition were discovered by chance in 1962. They are thought to originate from the second half of the 3rd c. A.D. They represent scenes from Greek mythology: Narcissus; Triumph

of Dionysos; Thisbe and Pyramus; Dionysos, Acme and Icarius; Poseidon and Amymone; Peneios, Apollo and Daphne; Hippolytus and Phaedra; Ganymede and the Eagle. Also to be seen: The Four Seasons, scenes from the grape harvest and hunting, geometric designs and animals including the moufflon. In order to appreciate fully these works of art consult the English version of notes by G.S. Eliades which is on sale at the custodian's office.

**House of Theseus** ⑫. Just a few steps towards the south-west the excavations under the guidance of Polish experts are still under way. Since 1966 remains of what is thought to have been the Roman governor's house have been carefully brought to light. Outstanding 4th c. mosaics have also been found here. The grandiose site gets its name from one of the mosaics, of Theseus killing the Minotaur. The 4th c. mosaic of Achilles the young hero being bathed for the first time is of particular interest because the style may have influenced the later Christian representations on icons and wall paintings of the first bath of the baby Jesus.

In the **House of Aion** ⑬, on the way

back from the House of Theseus to the House of Dionysos, there are more mosaics which were only discovered in 1983. They portray the handing over of the child Dionysos to the Silenus Tropheus, Leda and the Swan, the musical competition between Apollo and Marsyas, the beauty contest between Cassiopeia and the Nereids and the triumphant procession of the child Dionysos. Some of these are only partially intact.

**Castle of Forty Pillars** ⑭. *Saranda Kolones*, as the excavated and restored remains of this fort are called, is a testimony to the military architecture of the time of the early Crusades. It was destroyed in the 13th c.

**Harbour Fort** ⑮. The small harbour of Paphos with its tavernas rich in Mediterranean atmosphere is dominated by the Frankish castle. It was built

*Dionysos mosaics, Paphos*

in 1391 and reinforced by the Turks in 1592 into its present-day form as a solid stronghold. The British used it for salt storage. There are good views over the harbour from its roof.

**Panayia Limeniotissa** ⑯ was one of the early Christian basilicas. This triple-aisled building, length 52 m, width 19 m, is of 5th c. origin.

**The Centre** ⑰: *Ayia Kyriaki Chrisopolitissa, Pillar of St Paul, Gothic cathedral, early Christian basilica.* The Byzantine Ayia Kyriaki in the centre of Nea Paphos provides the visitor with a welcome landmark in this vast excavated area. A stone's throw away to the west is the Pillar of St Paul. This perhaps most historical of monuments from early Christian times had to be removed from its original site and fenced off to prevent souvenir-hunting tourists from scraping it down to its base. In A.D. 45 the Apostle Paul is said to have been bound to this very pillar by the pagan citizens of the town. In spite of this he later succeeded in converting the Roman governor to Christianity, thereby causing Cyprus, even if only temporarily, to be ruled by a Christian for the first time.

Between the Pillar of St Paul and the

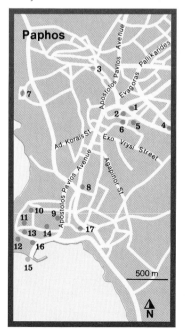

**Paphos**

Apostolos Pavlos Avenue
Palikarides
Evagoras

3
7
1
2
5
6
4
Ad. Koraïs St.
Exo Vrysi Street
Agapinor St.
Apostolos Pavlos Avenue
8
10
9
11
13 14
17
12 16
15

500 m

**N**

*Saranda Kolones, Kato Paphos*

Ayia Kyriaki the remains of a large three-naved Gothic cathedral built in 1300 can be seen.

The ruins of an early Christian basilica (4th c., altered in 6th c.) lie close by, around and under the Ayia Kyriaki. Being 53 m in length and 38 m wide it must have been one of the biggest in Cyprus. Four pink granite columns to the south of Ayia Kyriaki supported the roof of the basilica's eastern wing. Remains of the mosaic floors can still be seen.

Ideal combination of relaxation, sport and culture.

*Theos* and *Pelican*, fish restaurants on the harbour front;

*Hondros*, near the harbour; *Mandra Tavern*, 4 Dionysiou St.; *Pyramos Tavern*, 54 Ay. Anastasias St.; *Gorgona*, 10 Poseidon St.

 *Daphne Disco*, *Mayfair*, St Antonios St.

*Venus* (Cabaret), E. Pallikarides Ave.; *La Grotte de Paphos*, Ay. Antonios St.

Seaside resort with children's playground near the harbour; coast north of Paphos, especially *Coral* and *Lara Bay*.

 Saturday Market.

*Paphos Castle*

 June 28th St Paul's Day. Religious service in Nea Paphos, in which mass is celebrated by the Archbishop dressed in the full splendour of his Byzantine regalia, and assisted by all the bishops of the island; followed by a procession.

Greek dramas performed in ancient theatre (Odeon). Information at CTO.

Cypriot Handicrafts, 123 Makarios III Ave., Fitiodika embroidery, basketware, Turkish sweets.

 Cyprus Tourism Organisation, Information Office, 3 Gladstone Street, Ktima, tel. 061-32841; and Paphos airport, tel. 061-36833. Information on:

 **East of Paphos**

**Yeroskipos** Pop. 1750 (3 km)
To the east of Paphos lies the 'Sacred Garden of Aphrodite', *Hieroskipos*, from which Yeroskipos is derived. One of the two five-domed Byzantine churches in Cyprus which have survived the ravages of time stands here; the other is in Peristerona.

The *Ayia Paraskevi* lies in the centre of Yeroskipos (approaching from Paphos, turn right). The interior of the 11th c. church is decorated with 9th–14th c. frescos. When the church is locked the key is available from the shoemaker Georgios Achilleos who lives in the street south of the church. He will proudly point out the beautiful features of his church and show you a 15th c. icon, carried in processions, which is painted on both sides. Close by in a narrow village street there is a very good museum of folk culture in an 18th c. house.

---

### A special tip

Lokoum, the Turkish sweetmeat made from honey and butter, is available throughout the island, but the best is to be found in Yeroskipos.

---

**Palea (Old) Paphos/Kouklia** (12km)
To the east of Nea Paphos, partly below and partly in the middle of the village of

**Surroundings of Paphos**

Kato Pyrgos
Pomos    Kokkina
Cape    Khrysokhou
Arnaouti    Bay
Fontana
Amorosa
**Baths of**    Lachi
**Aphrodite**    Polis
Akamas    Prodhromi
Peninsula    Androuliko
Lara    Phasli    Lyso
Bay    Inia    Pano
Cape    Kannaviou    Panayia
Drepanum    Kathikas
Polemi
**Basilica**    Peyia    **Chrysorroyiatissa**
**of Peyia**    Maa    **Monastery**
Coral    Lemba    **Ayio's Neophytos**
Bay    **Monastery**    Ayios
Paphos(Ktima)    Yeoryios
Nea Paphos    Episkopi    Stavrokono
Yeroskipos    **Ayia**
**Paraskevi**
**Church**
**Palea**    Kouklia
**Paphos**
N
15 km    Petra tou Romiou

Kouklia, are the ruins of Palea Paphos, the Sanctuary of Aphrodite. All that remains of one of the most sacred sites of the ancient world is broken walls, grass-covered plinths, pieces of Roman mosaic floors, steps and column bases.

And yet the goddess of love has not been completely forgotten at her birthplace. Even in the last century the inhabitants of the region worshipped the Virgin Mary as *Panayia Aphroditissa!*

The Cinyrades used to rule here, successors of the legendary priest king Cinyras who allegedly introduced the cult of Aphrodite to Cyprus about 1200 B.C. It was here that the 12-km-long annual pilgrimage finished; this began in Nea Paphos for thousands of pilgrims from the whole of the ancient world whose goal was to participate in the famous four-day *Aphrodisia*. They included competitive games, a sea-bathing ritual, sacrifice and a grand closing ceremony involving the initiation of converts.

Palea Paphos with a former population of 20,000 used to be the religious centre of the whole of the island. Its end was brought about in the 4th c. A.D. by terrific earthquakes that destroyed the Shrine of Cypris, and by a decree of Emperor Theodosius (379–395) who ordered the closure of all heathen temples.

It was not until the 13th c. that the town prospered again, when it became the centre of the royal sugar-cane plantations under the Lusignans.

### 📷 Sightseeing

**The Frankish Castle** (*Manoir de la Covocle*) is of Lusignan origin but very little of it remains. Today there is an *epigraphic and archaeological museum* housed in some of the rooms dating from the Turkish period. It contains an impressive collection of local exhibits: tools and jewellery from the Chalcolithic period, ceramics from the Late Bronze

*Yeroskipos Church*

Age to the Graeco-Roman period, faience work imported from Egypt (6th c. B.C.), objects tooled from iron, ivory and silver, and 6th and 5th c. B.C. sculptures. The name of medieval Kouklia is said to be derived from this castle called Manoir de la Covocle. Nowadays Kouklia is a poor village with a population of about 1200.

## Sanctuary of Aphrodite

Only the remains of the north and south wings of the site, which were probably part of the adjoining area of the temple town, have been excavated to date. The sanctuary itself probably still lies buried.

The remarkable cone-shaped greenish-black stone, 1.25 m high, which today is in the museum in the Frankish Castle, was found in 1887 during excavations among the ruins to the north of the temple buildings, which had two extended colonnades to the south and east. Its position below the building level suggested that even during the various stages of rebuilding it was never moved. Being one of the oldest cult objects it was regarded as sacred. The villagers of Kouklia called it *Ayia Mawra*, 'Black Saint'. For centuries the mysterious magic of this primeval stone idol stood for the dark side of the goddess of fertility as ruler of the dead, an ancient role that the Olympian goddess inherited from her predecessor — the Great Mother who was worshipped throughout Asia Minor.

The most sacred object in the temple itself was a similar prehistoric cone,

*Mural in Neophytos Monastery*

white in colour. It has still not been discovered up to the present day. It is represented on Roman coins at the centre of a tripartite stand flanked by pillars and bordered by doves and stars (symbols of Astarte — a Syrian forerunner of Aphrodite).

You need to use your imagination to be able to envisage the vast area of this sanctuary — according to Virgil 'the temple of a hundred altars' — which was once covered in a forest of statues and amassed immeasurable riches during its existence of over a thousand years.

A copy of the famous mosaic of Leda with the swan (2nd/3rd c.) is on view at the spot where it was originally discovered, about 100 m from the sanctuary. The original is on display in the National Museum in Nicosia.

## Petra tou Romiou

5 km east of Palea (Old) Paphos where the coast road becomes most exciting and picturesque lies the legendary place where, in the words of Homer, Aphrodite, Greek goddess of love, beauty and spring, 'was born out of the soft sea foam at Paphos'. Nature has left a worthy monument to this event, a white limestone rock — Petra tou Romiou — in the deep blue sea. Should you choose to resist the temptation to bathe in the refreshing waters then you can enjoy the magical view from the tourist pavilion (where there is a restaurant).

## 🚌 North of Paphos

### Neophytos Monastery (9 km)

The monastery, north of Paphos, is situated above a ravine which stretches as far as the sea. It is named after its founder who settled here in a cave in 1159.

He later extended this cave, turned it into a church and dedicated it to the Holy Cross. He was joined by other settlers and several more cells were completed. In 1183 Neophytos had the walls of his first cave decorated. Some of these wonderful blue-based frescos were repainted in 1530; others are still in their original condition. They are without doubt some of the best examples of that time and are reminiscent of works of the school of Constantinople.

The monastery church which developed around the cave is a triple-naved building from the end of the 14th c. The wall paintings in the naves are of 15th c. origin and those in the apse thought to be 16th c.

## The Coast between Paphos and Cape Arnaouti

The coast north of Paphos as far as the Akamas peninsula is noted for its bathing beaches. The hilly hinterland, a unique vineyard and orchard interspersed with banana plantations and fields of early vegetables, is the home of prosperous villages which produce delightful wines.

Maa is reached via *Lemba*, where in 1981 tombs and houses from the period 3850–2760 B.C. were excavated. At *Maa-Palaeokastro* archaeologists have uncovered a settlement and palace belonging to Mycenaean settlers from the 13th c. B.C. Below this site is the magnificent sandy beach *Coral Bay*. A new holiday centre is being developed here.

**Basilica of Peyia.** It is no more than 9 km from Paphos to the picturesque hamlet *Peyia*. Here you turn left towards *Ayios Yeoryios* and 7 km further on you come across a small village by the sea.

*The wild west coast of Cyprus*

The 6th c. ruins of the *Basilica of Peyia* with its mosaic panels and beautiful marble capitals point to the former existence of an important town, which was called Drepanum in Roman times.

Travelling further north where the region is deserted and undeveloped you come to Lara Bay. Here there is a breeding centre for green turtles which are threatened with extinction. The animals raised at the centre are released into the sea when they reach a certain size. In 1983 the number released was 4605.

*Chrysorroyiatissa Monastery entrance*

An attractive scenic route takes in Kathikas, Inia, Phasli, Androuliko, Prodhromi and Polis.

## Khrysokhou Bay

Following a well constructed road for 39 km past the wine town of *Stroumbi* you come to *Polis* (population 1700), centre of the citrus-growing area. Polis is situated on the bay itself, an undeveloped region as far as international tourism is concerned. Freshly prepared seafood dishes are served in the tavernas of *Latsi*, a fishing village 3 km west of Polis.

In August the land shaded by olive trees around the so-called *Baths of Aphrodite* is transformed into a huge camp site. One wonders whether the Cypriot families on holiday here have come to seek eternal youth by bathing in the enchanted grotto where Aphrodite was surprised by Acamas.

If you walk the 6 km along the Bay of Khrysokhou from the tourist pavilion to *Fontana Amorosa* you will be rewarded by the fascinating landscape and quiet coves. The fountain of love is, however, rather disappointing. If you drink from it you are more likely to fall sick than fall in love.

A red flag flying at the beginning of the path means that British troops are on exercises in the area stretching as far as Cape Arnaouti. Walking is still permitted but is not very relaxing.

To the north of Polis the Bay of Khrysokhou is bordered by fruit and banana plantations and a sandy beach. You cannot go much further than Pomos. Nowadays Kokkina is a Turkish Cypriot enclave and the Green Line begins just past here.

## Chrysorroyiatissa Monastery (39 km)

This monastery, situated north-east of Paphos in the Troodos Mountains, was founded by the hermit Ignatius. The best route is via Polemi, Kannaviou and Pano Panayia, the birthplace of Makarios III. The house where he was born is now a museum. According to the legend, one day Ignatius caught sight of an unusual light. He approached it and found an icon of the Virgin Mary which he took with him into his cave. During this brief visitation the Virgin Mary told him to build a chapel on the slope of Royia (pomegranate) mountain close by his cave.

This chapel grew into a monastery. After periods of decline the monastery regained some of its former importance. The present-day building of 18th c. origin has a viewing terrace where the visitor can rest.

 Excellent dry wines are produced at the monastery.

# The Troodos Mountains

These lie in the 'Mid-West' of the island. Agriculture and forestry combine on the lower slopes to make them particularly attractive. Here the corn is still cut by hand and carried by mules to the barn. On the sparsely wooded upper slopes with the scattered flat-roofed houses you occasionally feel as if you are in Japan. The topography of these mountains is a fascinating mixture — rolling hills, wooded ravines and rugged scree-covered slopes. Mount Olympos, at 1953 m the highest mountain on the island, is surrounded between 1300 and 1725 m by the spa resorts of Platres, Troodos, Prodhromos and Pedhoulas. Increasing numbers of Cypriots and even visitors from Arab countries spend their summer holidays here. The numerous springs in this part of the Troodos range supply not only the whole island but also the mainland of the Middle East with excellent mineral water.

The entire forested area of the mountain range is state property. It consists of Aleppo pines, Corsican pines, golden oaks, plane trees, cedars, alders and strawberry trees. Hares and foxes abound and if you are lucky you may catch a glimpse of the odd moufflon. Eagles and ravens are not uncommon.

The many churches and monasteries with extremely beautiful wall paintings are well worth seeing. Some have already been described because they are more accessible from Nicosia, Larnaca or Paphos. They are the monasteries of Makheras (see page 36), Stavrouni (see page 42) and Chrysorroyiatissa (see page 70).

Two routes into the heart of the Troodos Mountains from both Nicosia and Limassol are to be recommended. The fastest from Nicosia is via Peristerona and Kakopetria to Troodos (60 km); the alternative is via Pedhoulas (70 km). Travelling from Limassol the shortest route to Platres is via Trimiklini (42 km); alternatively go via Kandou and Omodhos (55 km).

## Platres Alt. 1233 m

Platres, 68 km south-west of Nicosia and 42 km north-west of Limassol, is situated in the middle of the Troodos range and is easily accessible by a good, fast road. Platres is one of the most scenic mountain spa resorts in the Middle East and is ideally situated as a departure point for walks and excursions in this area. It has an ideal climate with hot dry days and cool nights. The mountain air scented with the aroma of pine is bracing, and the tranquillity far away from the hubbub of

the city is a welcome relief for nerves frayed by the pressures of urban life. If you can leave the sea and usual holiday bustle behind, you will discover that Platres is more relaxing than any other holiday resort on Cyprus. It must be added that there are numerous modest hotels and pensions here but only one luxury-class hotel. Its leafy terraces, extensive menu and large swimming pool will induce a feeling of well-being from the minute you arrive.

The village itself is a curious mixture of part British 'afternoon tea' atmosphere, part Greek villagem, and part international spa with its surprisingly multilingual population.

In July and August it gets quite busy here, when the Cypriot families and their many children come to the mountains to escape the summer heat. The larger towns on the coast then offer more distractions. The visitor who seeks more than good food, swimming, walking and reading should stay down there. Platres offers no other holiday activities, apart from horse riding and joining in the Platres Festival in September, which consists of 3-4 days of agricultural displays, folk dancing, plays, and horse and donkey races.

 *Forest Park, Edelweiss.*

 *Phidias, Caledonian.*

 *Andis.*

 in *Forest Park Hotel.*

 *Cyprus Tourism Organisation* (in summer; tel. 054-21316) in the main street of the resort. Information on:

## Mount Olympos Alt. 1952m
The summit of the highest mountain, which was once dedicated to Zeus and Aphrodite, can be reached in half an hour from Platres on an asphalted road which is very winding in places. The best time to visit Mount Olympos is at dawn or dusk. Despite the radar stations and T.V. antennae the view is breathtaking.

## Troodos Alt. 1725m
The highest resort on Cyprus is situated just below the summit of Mount Olympos like a giant sun terrace. In summer Troodos attracts numerous campers, and in winter, skiers. It is the only part of Cyprus for winter sports although the slopes are rather gentle and the descents not very long.

Directly below the small town of Troodos on the left is the entrance to the Archbishop's summer residence, for which the French poet Rimbaud carried and stacked bricks. A plaque at the rear entrance of the building commemorates Rimbaud's bricklaying.

 Ski slope, ski school, ski lift. Skiing is usually available from January to March. Gentle slopes. Skis can be hired from the *Cyprus Ski Club.*

 at *Dolphin Tourist Pavilion.*

4 guided walks. Brochures available from tourist office (CTO).

## Troodhitissa Monastery
Alt. 1555m
The monastery is situated about 8km north of Platres. It has a picturesque and very interesting church which was built in 1731 on the remains of an old 13th c. church. It contains valuable icons from the 16th c. which are of Italian influence. Annually on August 15th the main icon of Madonna Troodhitissa, which is covered in silver plate, is brought out into the open. It is placed on a stand under which believers crawl in order to share in the good fortune that this painting is supposed to bring. Another of the

monastery's treasures is the Holy Belt. Women who have not been granted children put the bronze-covered relic around their waists. In days gone by if a male child was born he was dedicated to serve in the monastery.

🏺 The monastery is renowned for the good-quality fruit grown in its orchards.

### Kykko Monastery Alt. 1270m

If you approach from the direction of Platres via Troodhitissa you come past the little town of Prodhromos to *Pedhoulas* which is famous for its cherry blossom and Sunday market. Here the wide tarmac road turns off and leads with many twists and turns to *Kykko* (18km).

Kykko, the most prosperous and famous of the monasteries on Cyprus, was founded by the settler Isaias, but after several fires nothing remains of the original building constructed between 1080 and 1118. However, an icon of the Virgin Mary, supposed to have been painted by the apostle Luke and to have rain-making powers,

*In the Troodos Mountains*

*Kykko Monastery*

survived the catastrophes. Kykko is a favourite spot for excursions and for pilgrims on August 15th (Assumption) and at weekends. Numerous souvenir shops and kiosks selling drinks and sweets turn the square in front of the monastery into a veritable fair.

The monastery buildings are all 19th and 20th c. The wall paintings in the monastery church and the roughly worked mosaics, glazed in gold, on the walls of the arcaded passages in the inner courtyards, are creations of the early 1980s. Artistically they are not very significant but they clearly illustrate how even today Cyprus's religious art is still firmly in the Byzantine tradition. On the other hand the exhibits in the monastery museum opposite the church are of great artistic worth.

### Throni tis Panayias Alt.1318m
The heights of Kykko (Throni tis Panayias) 2km from the monastery

became a national shrine as the final resting place of Archbishop Makarios III. Not far from the place where he trained and became a priest stands a black marble sarcophagus on which are engraved extracts from his speech to the UN in that fateful year 1974.

### Valley of the Cedars and Stavros tis Psokas
The visitor who is adventurous enough to travel further into the loneliness of the Troodos Mountains on a very winding unmade road from Kykko will find many pretty places to stop and have a picnic. The extensive Valley of the Cedars with over 30,000 legally protected trees lies 16km to the west of Kykko. 27km to the west and an hour and a half's drive from Kykko on unmetalled roads in the middle of the Paphos forest is the forest station Stavros tis Psokas, a place of particular beauty which is also famous for its moufflon reserve. This mountain sheep

— a powerful and splendid creature with a pale brown coat and curled ram-like horns — used to exist in large numbers in this area many years ago. After its numbers dropped to 15 in 1937 it was made a protected species with the result that today over 400 of these animals again live in the Troodos range.

Two thirds of the island's forests are administered from this forest station.

 Overnight accommodation available at forest station.

## Panayia tou Arakou at Lagoudhera

From Troodos you drive past the asbestos mines at Amiandos in the direction of Khandria and reach Lagoudhera after about 20 km. The road is uneven, narrow and winding, but because of the marvellous scenery you should take your time anyway.

The noteworthy church of Panayia tou Arakou, dating from 1192, conceals one of the oldest and best examples of Byzantine wall painting on Cyprus. The representations of Christ in the cupola — birth, baptism, burial and ascension — are only some of the impressive scenes.

The key to this church which has an overhanging protective roof is available in the neighbouring building which was formerly a monastery.

## Panayia Ayiasmati at Platanistasa

About 9 km further east of Panayia tou Arakou, past *Polystipos* famous for its hazelnuts and almonds, past *Alona* where the village street runs between leafy vines, lies Platanistasa, a charming place. The inhabitants soon notice that the visitor is looking for the key to Panayia Ayiasmati and send for the curator who is keen to accompany him to the church 5 km away. Marvellous frescos completed by an artist called Philippe Goul, 1494, depict scenes from the lives of Christ and Mary. The life-size saints are remarkable. The route from Platanistasa to Peristerona is uninterrupted (22 km). On a path marked in red you can walk to Lagoudhera in 2–3 hours.

*Cyprus is rich in church architecture*

## Kakopetria and Galata

Both these places are in the process of becoming overcrowded summer holiday resorts. They are only 48 km from Nicosia and 12 km from Troodos on the Karyotis river. The church of *Ayios Nikolaos tis Stegis*, 3 km south-west of Kakopetria, on the land of a study centre in a wild, romantic valley, is worth a visit. The church has been completely decorated with wall paintings; the oldest ones — the 'Raising of Lazarus' and the 'Procession into Jerusalem' — are from the 11th c. A shingle roof protects the tile-covered domed church.

### A special tip

If you feel hungry while in Kakopetria and Galata you should try the trout. The best trout in Cyprus are farmed in the Karyotis river.

## Panayia Phorviotissa-Asinou

Approximately 18 km north of

Kakopetria near the locality of Kato Koutraphas you leave the main road to Nicosia. In *Nikitari* you have to find the priest who keeps the key to the church of Asinou, Panayia Phorviotissa (5km), which stands alone in a wooded valley. The steep-pitched roof at first appears rather odd but the inside of the 12th c. building surpasses all expectations. It is not an exaggeration to count the Byzantine frescos of the church of Asinou among the best in Cyprus. It is not possible to describe even a small part of the painted church here. The following selection from the singularly well preserved series of paintings (mainly 12th-14th c.) should be mentioned: in the apse, behind the iconostasis, 'Mother of God with the Archangels Michael and Gabriel'; 'The Last Supper'; 'The Birth of Christ'; 'The Raising of Lazarus'; 'The Death of the Virgin'; 'The Last Judgement'.

## Other churches

If you have plenty of time you should visit the following churches: *Panayia Eleousa* in Galata, the monastery *Ioannis Lambadistou* at Kalopanayiotis and the *Panayia tou Moutoullas* near the resort of Moutoullas, famous for its mineral water.

*Nicosia, the Old City with St Sophia in the background*

# A brief look at the Turkish Occupied Zone

The countryside to the north of the Demarcation Line is equally attractive and rich in history. As a tragic result of the fighting in the summer of 1974 this region is totally inaccessible for Greek Cypriots, and foreign tourists can only visit it under certain conditions (see page 89).

The main sights of Northern Cyprus, described below, clearly show how both parts of this divided country share a common history.

## Nicosia Turkish: Lefkosa (Northern part); Pop. 30,000

The sights are marked on the map on page 33. From the only border crossing point at the old Ledra Palace Hotel you carry on straight ahead to the wide main road, Anatolu Avenue, then turn right again at the Kyrenia Gate into the Old City.

### 📷 Sightseeing

**St Sophia** (*Selimiye Mosque*) ⑮.*
Building began on this splendid Gothic cathedral, formerly the church where the Lusignans were crowned, in 1192 and continued in the 13th c. with the help of French craftsmen and artists. It was consecrated in 1326 amid much ceremony. The building has been damaged on several occasions by earthquakes, and by the local Greeks rebelling against the Catholic suppression of the Greek Orthodox Church. It was plundered by the Genoese in 1372, by the Mameluks in 1426 and by the Turks in 1570. In spite of this the cathedral remains a magnificent building. The beauty of the church is not impaired by the muezzins calling to prayer from the two minarets instead of the bells ringing from the tower. In fact the opposite is almost true. The ambitious interior, where the warm, white light gathers, may never have been so beautiful as it is today for in this cathedral, instead of the usual covering of Christian pictorial decoration, there is only a beautiful sea of carpets in every shade of red and, on the bare white columns, a few quotations from the Koran in Arabic script.

**Bedestan** (*St Nicholas*) ⑯. Bedestan is a Turkish word which means covered market. The Bedestan on the south side of St Sophia's Cathedral is a 14th c. Gothic church, unfortunately close to ruin, which was used in Turkish times as a market place for textiles, and later

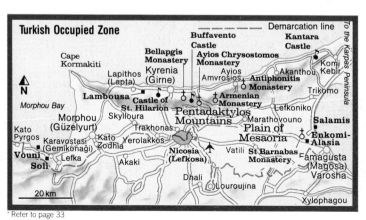

Turkish Occupied Zone — map showing Demarcation line, Cape Kormakiti, Lapithos (Lapta), Kyrenia (Girne), Lambousa, Castle of St. Hilarion, Bellapgis Monastery, Buffavento Castle, Kantara Castle, Ayios Chrysostomos Monastery, Ayios Amvrosios, Antiphonitis Monastery, Akanthou, Komi Kebir, Trikomo, Armenian Monastery, Lefkoniko, Pentadaktylos Mountains, Marathovouno, Salamis, Enkomi-Alasia, Plain of Mesaoria, Morphou Bay, Morphou (Güzelyurt), Skylloura, Trakhonas, Kato Pyrgos, Karavostasi (Gemikonaği), Kato Zodhia, Yerolakkos, Nicosia (Lefkosa), Vatili, St Barnabas Monastery, Famagusta (Magosa), Varosha, Vouni, Soli, Lefka, Akaki, Dhali, Louroujina, Xylophagou, Karpas Peninsula. 20 km. N.

as a granary.

St Nicholas is noteworthy as a typical example of Franco-Byzantine church architecture (pointed arches, cupolas). From the earlier Byzantine building a 12th c. wall painting of St Andrew has been preserved, and is still recognisable. Byzantine reliefs are also visible on the side facing the cathedral. Just a few yards away from St Sophia and Bedestan is the old *market hall* of Nicosia.

**Library of Sultan Mahmut** ⑰. It is situated opposite the east gate of St Sophia's Cathedral and is one of the most interesting buildings of Turkish origin remaining on Cyprus. The library was built in 1829 by Sultan Mahmut II and contains a collection of valuable manuscripts in Turkish, Persian and Arabic. The walls are decorated in Arabic script proclaiming the virtues of the Sultan.

**Museum of Stones** ⑱. In a 15th c. Venetian building evidence of the past in stone, including sarcophagi, tombstones and a well preserved Venetian heraldic lion, can be seen.

**Beuyük Han** ⑲. Originally a medieval building the Beuyük Han (the great caravanserai) was rebuilt in the 16th c. after the arrival of Mustafa Pasha, and furnished as an inn for travellers and traders. Every Cypriot had to pay a tax of 2 paras for the new building.

The Han has a picturesque arcaded courtyard with a small mosque in the centre.

**Kumarçilar Han** ⑳. This small caravanserai, also called 'the players' caravanserai', is just a few steps north of Beuyük Han. It was built in the 16th c. and modelled on the larger Beuyük Han.

**Venetian Column** ㉑. This former landmark of Venetian power stands in the centre of what is today called Atatürk Square. It is 8 m high and 80 cm wide, made of grey granite and said to originate from the temple at Salamis. A splendid Lion of St Mark used to crown the column but went missing at the time of the Turkish conquest in the 16th c.

**Mevlevi Tekke** ㉒. The former *Monastery of the Dancing Dervishes* was built in the 17th c. by Sultan Emine. The order, founded in the 13th c., was banned in 1925 by Kemal Atatürk. Since 1963 the building has housed a *Turkish Museum of Folk Art*. Minibuses to Kyrenia depart from the front of this building every few minutes (journey time 40 mins.).

**Famagusta** (Turkish: Magosa)

The history of Famagusta, which lies 61 km east of Nicosia, actually begins at Enkomi, an early predecessor of the town 13 km to the north, which first flourished in about 1550 B.C. An earthquake is thought to have destroyed Enkomi. Salamis, its dazzling successor, was founded at the beginning of the 12th c. B.C., possibly by the Trojan hero Teucer, and was to determine Cyprus's history throughout the centuries. After devastating earthquakes and repeated Arab attacks, the last inhabitants left the town in the early Middle Ages, to move 8 km further south to a new town to which they were to give the melancholy name Ammochostos. *Ammochostos* means 'hidden in the sand' and refers to the ruins of their old home which had been eroded by wind and sand.

Present-day Famagusta developed from Ammochostos. Scarcely more than a village at the time of the Lusignans (1192), its development, which began 100 years later with the fall of Acre (1291), led to its becoming the Venice of the Levant within a decade.

Famagusta's Golden Age was legendary but its fail seems no less legendary. In September 1570 only 5000 Venetian soldiers, under the

*Othello Tower, Famagusta*

command of Marc Antonio Bragadino, faced the Turkish army of 250,000 commanded by Lala Mustafa. In spite of the odds they withstood the siege of Famagusta for eleven months and only surrendered on August 1st 1571. Widespread slaughter followed in the city and Bragadino, the hero of Famagusta, was tortured for several days on the order of Lala Mustafa before being beheaded.

Under the new Turkish rulers the old Famagusta was not rebuilt but rather dismantled piece by piece into stones, columns and pillars by enterprising entrepreneurs, and shipped to Port Said, Alexandria and Suez as building material. What was left of the old Famagusta has been occupied up to the present day by the Turkish population. Until 1974 the Greek population lived in the modern part of Famagusta called *Varosha* (suburb) which was a modern holiday resort with a wonderful beach.

Since 1974 this former tourist centre has been a restricted area. If the hotel buildings were not destroyed in the fighting most of them have been subsequently rendered unusable. The name Varosha repeatedly crops up in the political discussions between Greek and Turkish Cypriots as a possible point of negotiation.

## 📷 Fortifications

All the town's sights are situated in the old part inside the formidable fortifications. Originally built by the Lusignans the walls, which are up to 17 m high in places and 7–9 m thick, were strengthened and extended by the Venetians in the 16th c.

The citadel, better known as the *Othello Tower*, on the seaward side of Old Famagusta, was later the seat of the Venetian governor. It owes its present name to Shakespeare who ensured its literary immortality by setting part of *Othello* there. The winged lion of St Mark on a white marble plinth above the tower entrance still looks in good condition today. The present shape of the citadel dates back to the alterations in 1492 by the Venetian Commander Foscarini. There is a marvellous view from the roof.

In the *Çambulat Bastion*, the south-east gate of the castle, there is a museum containing archaeological discoveries and exhibits of folk culture. Its name is derived from Emir Çambulat who died in the siege of Famagusta; the castle tower is his mausoleum.

*Cathedral of St Nicholas* (Lala Mustafa Mosque). This 14th c. cathedral, the most imposing on the island, is reminiscent of Rheims Cathedral in many of its features. The Lusignans were crowned kings of Jerusalem here. Since 1570 it has been used as a mosque.

*Palazzo del Provveditore*. In 1552 the Venetian governor built his residence opposite the cathedral as a sign of his worldly power. The Turkish conquerors made parts of it into a state prison. Only a portico with four granite columns still remains of the palace.

*Church of St Peter and St Paul* (Sinan Pasha Mosque). It is said to have been built in 1360 during Famagusta's Golden Age by a businessman, with the profits from a single business transaction. After the Turkish conquest it was turned into a mosque and then a granary until it was damaged by two earthquakes in the middle of the 16th c.

## Enkomi

Out of the bare plain 13 km north of Famagusta a ruined town emerges, its lowest strata stretching back to 2000 B.C. It is possibly *Alasia*, mentioned in ancient scripts as a copper centre. Rediscovered a few decades ago during the excavation of Enkomi village it disclosed priceless treasures. A well known example is the 12th c. B.C. statue of a horned god which ranks among the most beautiful exhibits in the Cyprus Museum. On the site of the excavation are the *House of Bronzes*, the *House of Columns*, the partly exposed town wall up to 3.5 m thick, the so-called *Building 18*, the remains of a palace and the *Sanctuary of the Horned God*.

## Salamis

Salamis, 8 km north of Famagusta, the 'Pompeii' of Cyprus, was the island's most important town in ancient times.

## 🏛 History

The town is thought to have been founded in 1181 B.C. by Teucer, the son of King Telamon from the Greek island of Salamis. Because of its favourable position, its excellent harbour and its busy trade in copper, corn, oil and salt, Salamis soon worked its way to the top of those city kingdoms which, even under foreign domination, retained their widespread regional independence in the Archaic period (about 700–475).

Evagoras, of the ancient royal family of the Teucrians, and whose regency (411–374) fell in the Persian era, also resided at Salamis. Despite heroic

*Right: Salami.*

resistance against the Persians he had to surrender after a year-long siege of Salamis in 379 B.C.

The Persians were succeeded by Alexander the Great, the Ptolemies and finally the Romans, who made Paphos the capital of the island, but under whom Salamis prospered in all its metropolitan grandeur. After an earthquake in the 4th c. A.D. Salamis was rebuilt by the Emperor Constantine and renamed *Constantia*. The part around the Basilica of St Epiphanius was secured by the Emperor Justinian II after the Arab attacks in the 7th c. and renamed *Nea Justinianopolis*. Following subsequent serious earthquakes the last inhabitants moved to Famagusta. The main part of the city of Salamis, which in Roman times encompassed 5.12 sq. km and registered a population of about 200,000, lies in ruins. It is the Roman era in the city's history, with its splendid buildings, which dominates the excavations we see today.

## 📷 Sightseeing

**Gymnasium.** This complicated site originates with a simple Hellenistic building, which was extended and altered during the Roman Empire and early Christian times. It served various purposes — part of it being a spacious bathing establishment which was still used as public baths after being altered in the Byzantine period. One continually comes across new rooms with remains of paintings and mosaics. There were even communal toilets with flushing water.

In the centre of the site lies the open courtyard (palaestra), still extremely impressive, which is surrounded on all four sides by marble Corinthian colonnades. The baths were housed in the south and north wings of the main building, and can be reached from the east colonnade via two vestibules with octagonal pools behind which were the heating chambers. Marble statues surround the empty swimming pools.

**Theatre.** Built towards the end of the 1st c. B.C. and destroyed by earthquakes in the 4th c. A.D. the theatre of Salamis was the biggest on the island. It held about 15,000 spectators. The auditorium consisted of more than 50 rows of seats and the stage was 40 m wide. Only 8 rows of seats are original; the others are reconstructions.

**Reservoir.** It is mainly of early Byzantine origin and was used for storing water that was carried by aqueduct from Kythrea. Two arches still remain of this water system, to the west of the nearby village of Ayios Serghios.

**Agora.** Once majestic marble-covered buildings stood around the giant market place (230 m x 55 m), one of the biggest in the ancient world. The remaining ruins are from the time of Augustus who had the square renovated. Considerable sections of the stone colonnades, which run in a southerly direction on both sides of the square, have been preserved. At the southern end of the square stood the *Temple of Zeus* of which the impressive podium can still be seen.

**Basilica.** Yet another superlative building to be found at Salamis was the 5th c. basilica, said to have been built by St Epiphanius. Measuring 58 m in length and 42 m in width it was the largest on the island and indeed one of the largest anywhere in Christendom. It was richly decorated with mosaics and originally consisted of a central nave flanked on each side by three aisles. At the eastern end of the middle one of the south-facing aisles there is a marble-covered tomb which is said to have contained the mortal remains of St Epiphanius. The structure adjoining this tomb was adapted as a church probably after the collapse of the

*Bellapais Abbey, Kyrenia*

basilica in the 7th c., and was later, presumably in the 9th c., vaulted by three cupolas. It was still in use long after the city of Salamis had been abandoned by its inhabitants.

**Tombs of the Kings.** Lying 1 km to the west of Salamis are the Tombs of the Kings from the Golden Age of the 8th/7th c. B.C. The finds made here are in the Cyprus Museum. A few artefacts are displayed in a small museum outside the town.

**Monastery of St Barnabas** *(Ayios Apostolos Varnavas).* A monastery dedicated to the apostle Barnabas, the patron saint of the island, 3 km away from his home town of Salamis where he met with a martyr's death. The triple-domed church is of 9th c. origin and until the 16th c. was the seat of the Archbishop of Cyprus.

100 m away from the monastery lies the apostle's unadorned chapel with the crypt where, according to legend, the bones of St Barnabas were found in the 5th c.

**Kantara Castle** Alt. 630 m
*Kantara* is situated 41 km north-east of Famagusta and is reached by a very winding road via Monarga (Turkish: Bogaztepe) and Yerani (Turkish:

Turnalar). From Kantara, a spa resort which today is largely abandoned, it is a further 3 km to Kantara Castle. This is one of the three proud medieval castles which stand on the summits of the northern mountain range, and is in considerably better condition than Buffavento. The fortifications and some cruciform vaulted living quarters from the 14th c. are particularly well preserved. Rainwater still collects in the cisterns of the west wing; the narrow steps directly adjacent to them perhaps lead to a secret exit. The northern part of the castle is without doubt the most beautiful, but take care when looking down from the narrow balcony.

## Karpas Peninsula

The peninsula of Karpas, a 70-km-long finger pointing north-east into the sea, offers not only a scenic landscape of dark forests and high dunes but also numerous historical buildings: the church of *Panayia Kanakaria* with mosaics from the 6th c., the Cathedral *Ayios Synesios* in Risokarpaso (Turkish: Dipkarpaz) and the *Monastery of St Andrew*. About 700 Greek Cypriots still live in the region of Risokarpaso, including their priest who is often to be seen in the Greek café.

## Kyrenia (Turkish: Girne)

Traditionally, ancient Kyrenia was founded by the Persian king Cyrus. But like so many places on the island this small town underwent a turbulent time during the reign of the Lusignans. In 1974 the first Turkish troops landed at this town, 26 km from Nicosia.

### 📷 Kyrenia Castle

The castle, a monumental fortification which forms the east side of the harbour, is unquestionably one of the most impressive old buildings of the entire island. Built in the 9th c. by the Byzantines, the castle was modified

*Left: Kyrenia harbour and castle*

and reinforced in 1208 by the Lusignans, and at the beginning of the 16th c. by the Venetians. To the left of the main guardhouse you reach the *Chapel of St George* which is built into the solid fortified wall. Stone coats of arms of the Lusignans are located above the main guardhouse and above the memorial to the Turkish admiral who took over the castle from the Venetians. From the top of the north-east tower you have a superb view.

In the *Shipwreck Museum* in the castle can be seen the remains of the hull of a trading ship which sank in 300 B.C. off Kyrenia. The cargo, part of which was salvaged, provided much information about its route, the crew, and the ship's technical properties. The ship had come from Samos and carried wine, almonds, milled cereals and amphoras; it had a speed of about five knots.

### 🚌 Excursions from Kyrenia

**St Hilarion Castle** Alt. 733 m. The well preserved castle of St Hilarion lies about 6 km south-west of Kyrenia on a steep mountain slope of the northern range. Originally a monastery which had developed around the dwelling of a Cypriot hermit, it was converted into a castle at the end of the 11th c. by the Byzantines. After the Lusignans had extended the building in the 13th and 14th centuries it was the Venetians who rendered the castle uninhabitable.

**Bellapais.** Above the town of Kyrenia, 5 km south-east, Bellapais rises out of a fragrantly green landscape at the foot of high cliffs and is one of the most significant and beautiful Gothic monuments still in existence in the Mediterranean region. The monastery was founded soon after the beginning of the Lusignans' rule (1192) by monks of the Augustinian Order. Its powerful abbots used to be influential at the royal court. The monastery's original name

was *Abbaie de la Pais* but it was later shortened to *Bellapais*. The oldest part still remaining is the church, built in the first half of the 13th c. The other undamaged monastery buildings, apart from the west wing, originate from the first half of the 14th c.

## Buffavento Castle Alt. 954 m

It is recommended that you visit Buffavento Castle from Nicosia only 22 km away, because the route from Kyrenia is much more difficult. Whichever way you approach it the last part, roughly a 20-minute climb, has to be covered on foot. Your efforts will be well rewarded for the view from these dizzy heights — on the one side the green coastal strip and the sea and on the other the entire plain of Mesaoria — is an unforgettable experience. Buffavento, which means 'blown by the winds', is the highest of the three castles (the others are St Hilarion and Kantara) which crowned the summits of the northern mountain range. All three were used as watchtowers by the Byzantines and modified into great fortresses by the Lusignans.

## Soli

Beyond the small town of Morphou (Turkish: Güzelyurt), 46 km west of Nicosia, you come to the bay of the same name. Directly beyond Karavostasi (Turkish: Gemikonagi) lies Soli, formerly one of the nine city kingdoms of the island and, on account of nearby copper mines, still a prosperous community in Roman and Byzantine periods. Its legendary founder is Acamas, the last of Aphrodite's Cypriot lovers.

Excavations have uncovered an early Christian basilica, a Roman theatre dating from the end of the 2nd c. B.C., and remains of the Aphrodite-Isis Temple, the oldest and most important temple of the town. Sculptures discovered here, including the beautiful Aphrodite of Soli, are displayed in the Cyprus Museum in Nicosia.

## Vouni

A few kilometres further west on the same Bay of Morphou you come to the remains of an important 5th c. B.C. royal residence, the *Palace of Vouni*, picturesquely situated on a plateau overlooking the sea. Countless rooms are grouped around a central courtyard. The site is reminiscent of Mycenaean palaces in Greece. The palace contains a Turkish bath, the oldest one known. In 380 B.C. the building was destroyed by fire. The royal family treasure was recovered undamaged by the archaeologists.

*Left: Restaurant with growing vines, Kyrenia*

# Useful things to know

## Before you go

### Climate

There are 268 days of cloudless sunshine and average rainfall is only 375 mm. Most rain falls in December and January. The air is dry and healthy. The thermometer reaches 33°C in the months of July and August, 26-27°C in the mountains and over 40°C on the particularly hot and dry Mesaoria Plain. In the coastal area high summer temperatures are moderated by a refreshing sea breeze. In the Eastern Mediterranean the highest sea temperatures for the whole Mediterranean are recorded; in August it reaches 28°C. Even in the coolest months of January and February it does not drop below 16°C.

### What to take with you

As far as holiday clothes are concerned they cannot be too light or airy; cotton clothes are better for the hot climate than man-made fibres. A change of swimwear and two or three casual but smart outfits, as well as comfortable footwear for wandering around the town, for excursions and evenings, are much more important than a cocktail dress and evening suit. You can safely leave these at home unless you are staying in one of the luxury hotels.

Owing to the powerful rays of the sun you are recommended to wear a good pair of sunglasses, to cover your head and to pack a suntan cream with a high protection factor. As not all of the beaches are sandy a pair of bathing shoes could be handy. Amateur photographers will save money buying film in Britain.

The churches in Cyprus are often quite dark inside. If you wish to see the many beautiful frescos in detail remember to take a torch.

In winter a coat and umbrella are necessary. In the Troodos mountains at this time of year it can snow, so warm clothing and strong footwear are essential. Forgetting to pack something important is no cause for alarm. You can buy almost everything here.

### First-aid kit

Most internationally common medicines are available in Cyprus. The chemists are recognisable in Cyprus by the red Maltese cross. To be on the safe side you should still take a small first-aid kit containing medicine for pain and fever relief, headache tablets, sleeping tablets if necessary, something for upset stomachs (which more often than not are attributable to the heat rather than the cooking oil), something for colds which can be caught by rapid change of climate, and sticking plaster. If you require special medicine this should be obtained before the journey. For your own security check your insurance cover abroad before your departure.

## Getting to Cyprus

**By air:** Cyprus can be reached in five hours. Several scheduled and charter flights link Europe with the island. Scheduled flights are to Larnaca only, charter aircraft also fly to Paphos.

**By sea:** There are boat and ferry crossings from Greece, Israel, Syria, Lebanon and Egypt to the ports of Limassol and Larnaca.

There is no airport tax. The tax for sea ports is £1 CY.

### Taking a car

Right-hand drive vehicles can be used for 3 months on Cyprus without being subject to tax. As the International Green Card is not valid, temporary third party insurance should be taken out on arrival.

## Immigration and Customs Regulations

There are no particular requirements for the Republic of Cyprus. British and American citizens require a full valid passport.

Items for personal use only may be imported duty-free. In addition there are the following personal travel allowances: 200 cigarettes or 50 cigars or 250 g tobacco, ½ litre of spirits and ¼ litre of perfume.

## Important Note

The Greek Cypriot Government in Nicosia has declared it illegal to enter the Turkish Republic of Northern Cyprus. Visitors entering via the ports of Famagusta, Kyrenia and Karavostassi or via Erçan airport are not allowed to cross into the southern part of the island.

## Demarcation Line

The island is divided from east to west from Famagusta Bay to Morphou Bay by the so-called Attila Line or Green Line. Neither Greek nor Turkish Cypriots are allowed to cross the line and it is guarded by UN peace-keeping forces. The authorities of the Republic of Cyprus allow foreigners a one-day visit but no overnight stay in the Northern part of the island. The only crossing-point is the former Ledra Palace hotel in Nicosia. It is open daily from 7.30 a.m. to 6 p.m. Visas for a one-day visit are issued on the spot by the Turkish Cypriot administration on presentation of a passport and payment of £1 CY. You must insist on the issue of a separate form for this visa as well as for entry and departure stamps as Greece refuses admission to holders of passports with Northern Cyprus entries.

## During your stay

### Camping

The CTO (Cyprus Tourism Organisation) supervises the following camp sites:

- *Polis*, under eucalyptus trees;
- *Troodos*, opposite the former Hotel Pingos, in a pine wood;
- *Forest Beach Camping*, near Larnaca;
- *Ayia Napa Camping Site*.

A limited number of restaurants have permission to allow camping in their grounds if they have proper facilities. Unofficial camping is not allowed but a friendly word with a farmer or owner of a beach taverna might assist in getting your own site. Caravans and camper buses can be hired — information from tourist offices.

## Currency and Banks

The Cypriot currency is the Cypriot pound (£ CY). There are 100 cents to the pound. Banknotes are in denominations of £10 CY, £5 CY and £1 CY as well as 50 cents. Coins include ½,1,2,5,10 and 20 cents. (£1 CY = £1.20 sterling/ £1 sterling = 84 cents approximately at date of going to press.) Bank opening times are Monday to Saturday from 8.30 or 9 a.m. until noon. Some banks offer a foreign exchange service especially for tourists from 3.30 to 5.30 p.m. Money can be changed at the airport on arrival and departure. Eurocheques may be cashed and the standard credit cards are accepted in most hotels and many shops.

There is no limit to the amount of foreign currency or traveller's cheques that can be brought in. Should one wish to take back currency in excess of $500 U.S. then this should be declared on arrival. A maximum of £50 in Cypriot currency may be brought in.

You cannot take more than £50 CY out of the country. Currency in excess of $500 U.S. must be declared. It is forbidden to export antiques without a licence.

## Electricity

220-240 volts AC/DC. Plugs are three-pinned.

## Opening times
### Museums and Archaeological Sites

These vary according to season and are all different. Precise information can be found in the pamphlet '9,000 years of History and Culture' which is available free of charge from offices of the Cyprus Tourism Organisation (for address see page 91). Information can also be obtained from the ticket offices of archaeological sites and museums. The hotel reception can usually be of assistance in offering further details.

### Shops

In summer they are generally open from 8 a.m. to 1 p.m. and from 4 to 7 p.m., except Wednesday and Saturday afternoon.

## Photography

The use of a light filter is recommended. It is forbidden to photograph the Demarcation Line (Green Line) and its enclosures as well as all military installations.

## Post, Telephone

Postal services to Europe take 4–6 days and are all by air mail.

You can dial direct to Britain by using the national code 0044 and dropping the first nought of the area code (e.g. Norwich 0044-603-), followed by the number required.

Area codes on Cyprus are: Limassol 051, Nicosia 02, Larnaca 041, Paphos 061.

You can also dial direct to Cyprus from Britain. The code is 010 357 + area code.

Public telephones accept 5 and 10 cent coins. Calls connected via the hotel reception are considerably dearer than from call boxes.

Post Office opening times: Monday to Saturday 7.30 a.m.—1.30 p.m.

## Souvenirs

It is not easy to give advice on what to bring back. A wide selection of genuine and representative objects of Cypriot folk art is available from branches of *Cypriot Handicrafts*: Nicosia, Laika Yitonia and 186 Athalassa Ave.; Limassol, 25 Themidos St.; Larnaca, 6 Cosma Lysioti St.; Paphos, 123 Makarios III Ave. Here you will at least get some original ideas and a definite price guide for your shopping trips.

## Time

Cyprus is two hours ahead of GMT.

## Tipping

In addition to the 10% service charge and 3% tourist tax a tip is usually given in restaurants and hotels. Taxi drivers should also be given a small tip.

## Transport in Cyprus

**Buses** are extremely cheap (average fare 1.5 cents per mile) and most places can be reached in this way. Departure times may vary especially if you are not on the main route. The buses stop mostly on request.

**Car hire** is very reasonable, for example a Volkswagen Golf in the high season costs about £13 CY per day with unlimited mileage. The daily rate reduces slightly for longer periods of hire. You must be 21 and have a full driving licence.

Four star petrol costs 26 cents per litre, two star costs 24 cents and diesel 9 cents per litre. Do not forget that petrol stations close at 1 p.m. on Saturdays.

The *Cyprus Automobile Association* (CAA) is at 30 Homer Avenue, Nicosia (tel. 02-452521).

Cyprus has a good road network and most parts are accessible by car. Car ownership is high; consequently both town and country roads are busy. A motorway already exists between Nicosia and Limassol and another is planned between Nicosia and Larnaca.

## Taxis

There are two different types — service taxis and normal taxis; both are good value. Service taxis run chiefly between the main towns and have between four and seven seats. As the fare is divided between the passengers you can travel about 33 miles for £1 CY. Mini-buses travel along fixed routes and are free. They collect passengers and take them where they want to go within the town. If you choose an individual taxi-ride you will in future be able to read the state-controlled fare from the meter. A 5km trip costs about £1 CY.

## Traffic regulations

In Cyprus vehicles travel on the left.

Speed limits: in town 30m.p.h./ 45km p.h.; out of town 50m.p.h./ 75km p.h.

Particular care is required in the narrow side streets and on the winding roads in the Troodos Mountains. Road signs and signposts are in Greek and English.

## T.V., Radio and Newspapers

Both radio and T.V. broadcast English programmes. Imported English newspapers are available and there are the local daily *Cyprus Mail* and the *Cyprus Weekly*.

## Youth Hostels

There are youth hostels at:

Nicosia, 13 Prince Charles Street (tel. 02-444808);

Limassol, 120 Ankara Street (tel. 051-63749);

Paphos, Eleftherios Venizelos Avenue Ktima, tel. 061-32588);

Troodos (tel. 054-15429) and at the Forest Centre, Stavros tis Psokas (tel. 074-17454).

## Important Addresses
### Diplomatic and Consular Offices
#### In U.K.

*Cyprus High Commission,*
93 Park Street,
London W1Y 4ET; tel. (01) 499 8272.

#### In Cyprus

*British High Commission,*
Alexander Pallis Street, PO Box 1978
Nicosia; tel. (02) 473131.

### Airlines

*Cyprus Airways,*
Euston Centre, 29-31 Hampstead Road,
London NW1; tel. (01) 388 5411.

## Tourist Information
### In U.K.

*Cyprus Tourism Organisation,*
211/213 Regent Street,
London W1R 8DA; tel. (01) 734 9822.

### In Cyprus

*Headquarters of Cyprus Tourism Organisation,*
18 Th. Theodotou Street,
Nicosia; tel. (02) 443374.

*Branches of CTO:*

Laiki Yitonia, Nicosia; tel. (02)444264
Ayia Napa; tel (037) 21796.
Larnaca, Democratias Square; tel. (041) 54322, and Larnaca Airport; tel. (041) 54389.
Limassol, 27 Spyron Araouzous Street; tel. (051) 62756.
Paphos, 3 Gladstone Street; tel. (061) 32841, and Paphos Airport; tel. (061)36833.
Platres, in Pano Platres; tel. (054) 21316.

Opening times vary. There will certainly be someone on duty between 9 a.m. and 1 p.m. and between 4 and 6 p.m. Monday to Friday.

In CTO offices street maps are provided free of charge together with further brochures on hotels, restaurants etc., and of course friendly advice and information is always available — in English! Road maps can be purchased at bookshops. To find out what is on you should read *Time Out* and *Cyprus This Week — Tourist Guide.*

## Useful words and phrases

Although English is widely understood and spoken in Cyprus, the visitor will undoubtedly find a few words and phrases of Greek very useful. There is no standard system of transliteration of the sounds of Greek into Roman script. In the examples given below an approximate pronunciation only is given.

### The Greek alphabet

| | | | | | | | | | |
|---|---|---|---|---|---|---|---|---|---|
| A | α | Alpha | I | ι | Iota | P | ρ | Rho |
| B | β | Beta | K | κ | Kappa | Σ | σ | Sigma |
| Γ | γ | Gamma | Λ | λ | Lambda | T | τ | Tau |
| Δ | δ | Delta | M | μ | Mu | Y | υ | Upsilon |
| E | ε | Epsilon | N | ν | Nu | Φ | φ | Phi |
| Z | ζ | Zeta | Ξ | ξ | Xi | X | χ | Chi |
| H | η | Eta | O | ο | Omicron | Ψ | ψ | Psi |
| Θ | θ | Theta | Π | π | Pi | Ω | ω | Omega |

In the pronunciation guide below the following should be noted:
gh = a 'hard' g, as in go; dh = th in this; th = th in thick; kh = approximately the sound of ch in the Scottish word loch. Greek uses a semi-colon for a question mark.

| | | | |
|---|---|---|---|
| please | parakaló | Bank | trápesa |
| thank you | efkharistó | Railway station | stathmós |
| yes/no | ne or málista/óchie | Exchange Office | saráfiko |
| excuse me | me sinkhoríte | Police Station | astinomíkotmima |
| do you speak English? | omelíte anglaiká? | Public telephone | tiléfono |
| I do not understand | dhem katalamvéno | Information office | ghrafíopliroforíon |
| good morning/ | kaliméra | Doctor | yatrós |
| afternoon | | Chemist | farmakío |
| good evening | kalispéra | toilet | tooaléta |
| good night | kalí níkhta | ladies | yinekón |
| good bye | adío | gentlemen | andhrón |
| how much? | póso káni? | engaged | katiliménos |
| a single room | Dhomátio mé éna kreváti | free | eléftheros |
| a double room | Dhomátio mé dhio krevátia | entrance | isodhós |
| | | exit | eksodhós |
| with bath | mé bánio / lutró | today / tomorrow | símera / ávrio |
| I should like | thaíthela | Sunday / Monday | kiriakí / dheftéra |
| the bill, please | to loghariasmós parakaló | Tuesday / Wednesday | tríti / tetárti |
| everything included | óla simberilamvano- ménoo | Thursday / Friday | pémpti / paraskeví |
| | | Saturday / holiday | sávato / skholí |
| open / shut | aniktós / klistós | 0 midhén | 8 okhto |
| where is ... street? | pu iné to i odhós? | 1 énas / éna | 9 ennéa |
| ... square? | i platía? | 2 dhío | 10 dhéka |
| how far? | póso makhriá? | 3 tría | 11 éndheka |
| left | aristerá | 4 téssera | 12 dódheka |
| right | dheksiá | 5 pénde | 20 íkosi |
| straight on | katefthían | 6 éksi | 50 ekató |
| Post Office | takhidhromío | 7 eftá | |

Basket weaving

94

# Index

*Paphos harbour and castle*

Original German text: Heinz Peter Gückeritz. English translation: Angela Saunders. Cartography: Gert Oberländer.
Illustrations:
Pages 28, 32, 41, 42, 44, 47, 62, 74 by courtesy of Cyprus Tourism Organisation.
Pages 1, 3, 4, 8, 30, 56, 64, 65, 67, 75, 86, 93 by courtesy of Cypriana Holidays, London.
Pages 79, 81, 83, 84 Travel Trade Photography.
Pages 9, 11, 18, 19, 23, 25, 27, 31, 34, 37, 50, 55, 61, 63, 76, 94 Cyprus Slide Library, Dali Nicosia, Cyprus.
Pages 20, 21 Cyprus Museum, Nicosia, Cyprus.
Series editor — English edition: Alec Court.

The publishers have made every endeavour to ensure accuracy but can accept no responsibility for errors and omissions and their consequences. They are, however, always grateful to be notified of any inaccuracies.

Printed in Italy

ISBN 0-7117-0356-6